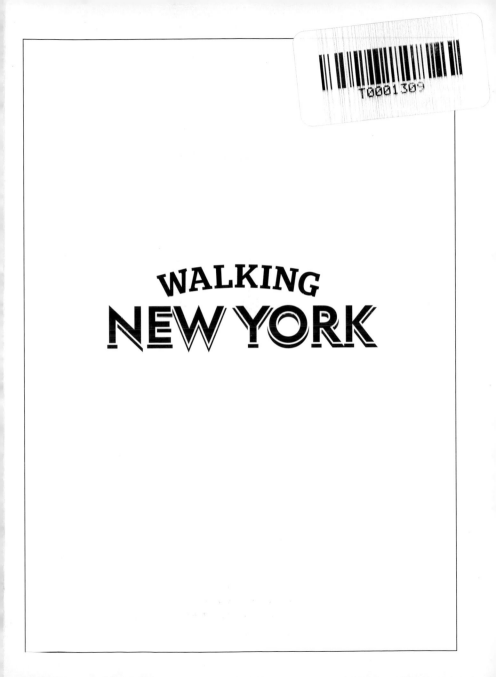

WALKING
NEW YORK

WALKING
NEW YORK

THE BEST OF THE CITY

Katherine Cancila

NATIONAL GEOGRAPHIC

Washington, D.C.

WALKING
NEW YORK

CONTENTS

PART 1

PAGE 12
WHIRLWIND TOURS

PART 2

PAGE 36
NEW YORK'S NEIGHBORHOODS

PART 3

PAGE 174
TRAVEL ESSENTIALS

Previous pages: Washington Square Park; left: Manhattan Bridge; right: doll from the Museum of the City of New York; above right: the Metropolitan Museum of Art; bottom right: Brooklyn Heights Promenade

Introduction

The first time I walked New York was with my uncle Buck. I was about six. He lived in Stuyvesant Town—known as Stuy Town and named for Peter Stuyvesant, the last director general of the Dutch colony of New Amsterdam. I remember the challenge of striding down the sidewalk, navigating the endless surge of humanity that came toward me. Later, I lived a stone's throw from Stuy Town, across from Tompkins Square Park. I spent hours on summer Saturdays sitting in the park, a tourist in my own neighborhood.

New York is the sum of its neighborhoods and the expression of endless waves of usually temporary citizens who come to make their mark and then move on. It is a city of and for walkers. Gawk at the ground-to-sky buildings—they seem more imposing and stylish here than in any other great world city. Snack at a corner street cart or sit in one of New York's hundreds of parks.

New York on a summer's day: Behind Central Park rise some of the art deco buildings that distinguish Midtown Manhattan.

Make this book your companion. It celebrates the art of the New York walk and abundantly delivers the how and where of doing it well. Want to do a whirlwind tour in a day? We have it. With kids? That, too. And, most important, we recognize what is becoming true of cities everywhere. You don't really visit a city; you visit its neighborhoods. This guide is engineered with that in mind—the key to a place whose bustling core measures just 34 square miles (88 sq km) and probably has more must-sees than any other city on the planet.

Keith Bellows

Former Editor in Chief, National Geographic Traveler *magazine*

Visiting New York

Few cities rival New York for cultural diversity, vibrant street life, world-class art and music, and sheer excitement. Much of this energy is packed into a narrow island just over 13 miles (21 km) long, so finding your feet can be a challenge.

New York Neighborhoods

It makes sense to approach Manhattan neighborhood by neighborhood, since each has a special character and attractions. If history is your thing, head for the southern tip of Manhattan to get a feeling of the city's preeminence as a trading port, then as a destination for European immigrants. Savor its literary past by strolling the tranquil streets of Greenwich Village, or track down the alternative spirit still alive in the East Village. Art lovers should zero in on the museums of the Upper East Side, head up to Harlem for Latino culture, and dip into glorious medieval art at The Met Cloisters. For visitors with more time, Brooklyn's superb museums, Prospect Park, and Botanical Garden beckon, along with great eateries.

New York Day-by-Day

Open every day (with some exceptions for major holidays) American Museum of Natural History, Central Park Zoo, Empire State Building, the Tenement Museum, Madame Tussauds, the Museum of Modern Art (MoMA), the National Museum of the American Indian, Rockefeller Center, St. Patrick's Cathedral, the Statue of Liberty, and Ellis Island.

Monday Most museums are closed except for those above and the Merchant's House Museum, Solomon R. Guggenheim Museum, and the Jewish Museum.

Tuesday The Brooklyn Museum, the Merchant's House Museum, Solomon R. Guggenheim Museum, The Studio Museum in Harlem, and the Whitney Museum of American Art are closed.

Wednesday The Jewish Museum, the Merchant's House Museum, the Metropolitan Museum of Art (The Met) and The Studio Museum in Harlem are closed.

Thursday The Museum of the City of New York is open until 9 p.m.; the National Museum of the American Indian is open until 8 p.m.

Friday The Morgan Library & Museum is closed. The Met is open until 9 p.m., MoMA until 8 p.m.

Saturday MoMA is open until 7 p.m.; The Met is open until 9 p.m.; the Jewish Museum is free.

The quiet streets of Greenwich Village break with the grid pattern of the rest of Manhattan and offer a wide range of independent shops and restaurants.

Taking a Break

Walking can get tiring, so note the places on your route where you can take a break. There are tiny parks and green spaces just off some main drags and big public areas such as Rockefeller Plaza and the David Rubenstein Atrium at Lincoln Center. Or hop on a bus to get a rest while seeing the sights.

Enjoying New York for Less

Sometimes there are free performances on offer. At Lincoln Center's David Rubenstein Atrium, for example, concerts of all kinds are presented every weekly. Drop by its information hub to find out about these and about free recitals by students from the Juilliard School. During the summer "Shakespeare in the Park" plays at the Delacorte Theater in Central Park. Tickets are free online or beginning at noon at the theater *(shakespeareinthepark.org)*. Most Broadway theaters also sell discounted standing-room-only tickets just before a show. Some museums have free entry at certain times, such as MoMA on Friday evenings. For visiting five of the major attractions, a City Pass *(citypass .com/new-york)* saves both money and time waiting in line.

Using This Guide

Each tour—which might be only a walk or might take advantage of the city's public transportation as well—is plotted on a map and has been planned to take into account opening hours and the times of day when sites are less crowded. Many end near restaurants, theaters, or lively night spots for evening activities.

Whirlwind Tours

Whirlwind Tours are for people who have only a day or a weekend to spend in the city and want to be sure that they see the best of the best. Choose your tour based on your time and interests: One Day; Weekend (Day 1 & Day 2); For Fun; and With Kids (Day 1 & Day 2).

Site Descriptions
For the For Fun and With Kids Tours, key sites spreads following the maps provide descriptions of all the sites and practical information for visitors.

Tips For the Day and Weekend Tours, a Tips spread following the itinerary map provides insider information on detours from the key sites, extra places to see, nearby cafés and restaurants, and ideas for adapting the tours to suit your interests.

Neighborhood Tours

The nine neighborhood tours each begin with an introduction, followed by an itinerary map highlighting the key sites that make up the tour and detailed key sites descriptions. Each tour is followed by an "in-depth" spread showcasing one major site along the route, a "distinctly" New York spread providing background information on a quintessential element of that neighborhood, and a "best of" spread that groups sites thematically.

Itinerary Map A map of the neighborhood shows the locations of the key sites, subway stations, and main streets.

Captions These briefly describe the key sites and give instructions on finding the next site on the tour. Page references direct you to full descriptions of the key sites on the following pages.

Route Dotted lines link the key sites.

Price Ranges for Key Sites

$	$1–$5
$$	$6–$11
$$$	$12–$18
$$$$	$19–$25
$$$$$	More than $25

Prices Ranges for Good Eats (for one person, excluding drinks)

$	Under $20
$$	$20–$35
$$$	$35–$50
$$$$	$50–$80
$$$$$	More than $80

Key Sites Descriptions Following the order of the tour, these provide a detailed description and highlights for each site, plus address, website, phone number, entrance fee, days closed, and nearest subway station.

Good Eats Refer to these lists for a selection of cafés and restaurants along the tour.

PART 1

Whirlwind Tours

New York in a Day

Visit the most famous building, shop in a favorite store, stroll in the city's greenest space, and join the Times Square party.

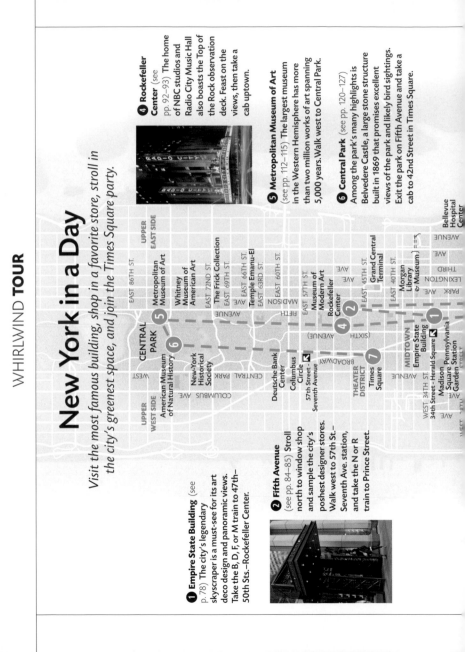

❶ Empire State Building (see p.78) The city's legendary skyscraper is a must-see for its art deco design and panoramic views. Take the B, D, F, or M train to 47th–50th Sts.–Rockefeller Center.

❷ Fifth Avenue (see pp. 84–85) Stroll north to window shop and sample the city's poshest designer stores. Walk west to 57th St–Seventh Avenue. Take the N or R train to Prince Street.

❹ Rockefeller Center (see pp. 92–93) The home of NBC studios and Radio City Music Hall also boasts the Top of the Rock observation deck. Feast on the views, then take a cab uptown.

❺ Metropolitan Museum of Art (see pp. 112–115) The largest museum in the Western Hemisphere has more than two million works of art spanning 5,000 years. Walk west to Central Park.

❻ Central Park (see pp. 120–127) Among the park's many highlights is Belvedere Castle, a large stone structure built in 1869 that promises excellent views of the park and likely bird sightings. Exit the park on Fifth Avenue and take a cab to 42nd Street in Times Square.

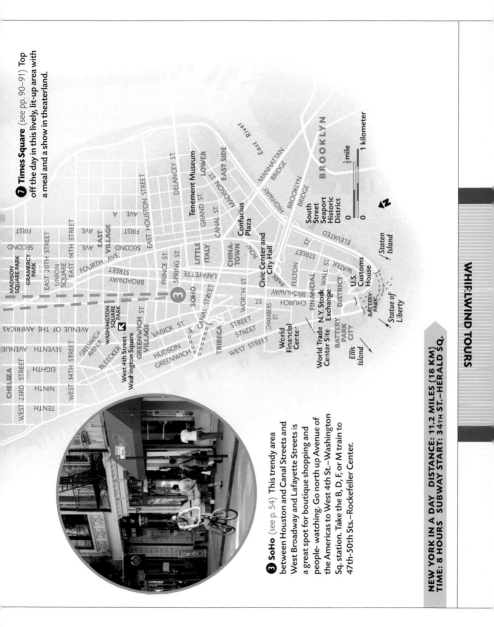

7 Times Square (see pp. 90–91) Top off the day in this lively, lit-up area with a meal and a show in theaterland.

3 SoHo (see p. 54) This trendy area between Houston and Canal Streets and West Broadway and Lafayette Streets is a great spot for boutique shopping and people-watching. Go north up Avenue of the Americas to West 4th St.–Washington Sq. station. Take the B, D, F, or M train to 47th–50th Sts.–Rockefeller Center.

NEW YORK IN A DAY DISTANCE: 11.2 MILES (18 KM)
TIME: 8 HOURS SUBWAY START: 34TH ST.–HERALD SQ.

Tips

These iconic New York sights are the best of the best. All are described elsewhere in the book; refer to the cross-references for detailed information. Here you have additional tidbits on visiting these major sights when you have limited time and suggestions for additional sights nearby and places to eat.

❶ Empire State Building (see p. 78) Even if you don't like heights and won't go to the viewing platform, pop in to the Empire State Building's art deco ■ **ENTRANCE LOBBY**. The marble-lined room has been recently restored and includes a fabulous wall relief of the building superimposed onto a map of New York State. After enjoying

Paley Park is an unexpected, secluded niche where you can escape the street for a while.

the great views from the 86th-floor balcony, walk the dense, block-long stretch of ■ **KOREATOWN** *(32nd St. between Fifth Ave. and Broadway)*, known for its restaurants, karaoke bars, and other small businesses. For some shady quiet, take a rest in ■ **GREELEY SQUARE** *(Broadway and West 32nd St.)*.

❷ Fifth Avenue After window shopping at some of the world's most famous stores, escape the Midtown crowds at ■ **PALEY PARK** *(53rd St. between Fifth and Madison Aves.)*, a concrete oasis tucked in between two buildings. A 25-foot (7.6 m) wall with a cascading waterfall, scattered patio furniture, and a concession stand add to its appeal. If it's raining, take shelter in ■ the **ST. REGIS HOTEL**'s grand atrium *(2 East 55th St., at Fifth Ave.)*, with its regal lounges and sumptuous Astor Court restaurant.

❸ SoHo (see p. 54) If your kids have lots of energy, let them blow off steam in the spacious ▪ **Vesuvio Playground** (*Spring St. between Sullivan and Thompson Sts.*), which is bordered with outdoor tables and benches. There are also a good number of casual and affordable lunch options nearby.

❹ Rockefeller Center (see pp. 92–93) During the summer, catch free morning performances by world-famous artists, such as Lizzo and Maroon 5, held by the ▪ **Today Show** at Rockefeller Plaza (*southwest corner of 49th St. and Rockefeller Plaza*). If you want to sample some classic New York ▪ **street food**, then try the carts selling cheap and delicious Middle Eastern fare that dot the street corners between Park and Sixth Avenues and 42nd and 56th Streets. Go to *newyorkstreetfood.com* for information on the most popular carts.

❺ Metropolitan Museum of Art (see pp. 112–115) Craving a less crowded corner of The Met during the hot summer months? Head to the fifth floor ▪ **Cantor Roof Garden Bar**, which hosts a small bar and has excellent views of Central Park.

❻ Central Park (see pp. 120–127) If you're with kids, head to the

CUSTOMIZING **YOUR DAY**

In spring and summer months, when it stays light until early evening, it's best to visit The Met before Central Park in order to see as much as possible before closing time. In the fall and winter, however, it becomes dark and cold far earlier, so be sure to get to Central Park by 3 p.m. in order to see the park in daylight and The Met before it closes.

▪ **Hans Christian Andersen Statue** (*by Conservatory Water*) where, on Saturday afternoons during summer, there are readings of Hans Andersen's much loved stories. Birdwatchers should visit ▪ **The Ramble** (*mid-park by 79th St.*), a 37-acre (15 ha) wood, home to more than 250 bird species.

❼ Times Square (see pp. 90–91) Commune with the ghosts of writers while sipping a delicious pre-dinner drink at the storied literary haunt, ▪ **The Algonquin** hotel (*59 West 44th St., between Fifth and Sixth Aves.*). As you cross Times Square, look for the old *New York Times* building's famous ▪ **tickertape** to catch up on the day's news. For dinner, check out ▪ **Sardi's** (*234 West 44th St., tel 212/221-8440, $$$$*), which offers a lively dining experience within caricature-covered walls, with a signature dish of steak tartare prepared at your table.

WHIRLWIND TOURS

New York in a Weekend

Midtown & Central Park

Intersperse the most popular sites with moments of peace and quiet.

④ Museum of Modern Art (see pp. 96–97) Among the world's most significant collections of modern art, MoMA houses Vincent van Gogh's "The Starry Night" and Andy Warhol's "Campbell's Soup Cans." Retrace your steps and continue north on Fifth Avenue.

③ St. Patrick's Cathedral (see pp. 93–94) One of the country's largest and most famous Catholic cathedrals, St. Patrick's offers a break from the Midtown landscape and the chance of a quiet moment. Continue north on Fifth Avenue to 53rd Street and turn west.

② Rockefeller Center (see pp. 92–93) Landmark art deco buildings and sculptures, along with nearly 150 places to shop and eat, make this complex a top destination for locals and tourists alike. Walk east on 49th Street to Fifth Avenue and head north.

⑤ Central Park (see pp. 120–127) Push past the horse-drawn carriages and make a beeline for the wide, tree-lined walkway known as The Mall, which starts mid-park at 66th Street. When you leave the park, take a cab downtown to 42nd Street in Times Square.

Map labels:

- American Museum of Natural History
- New-York Historical Society
- CENTRAL PARK WEST
- COLUMBUS
- Lincoln Center for the Performing Arts
- Time Warner Center
- Columbus Circle
- WEST 57TH STREET
- WEST 54TH STREET
- WEST 51ST STREET
- WEST 48TH STREET
- BROADWAY
- THEATER DISTRICT
- WEST 42ND ST.
- Times Square
- CENTRAL PARK
- EAST 76TH STREET
- EAST 72ND ST.
- Metropolitan Museum of Art
- Whitney Museum of American Art
- The Frick Collection
- EAST 69TH ST.
- EAST 66TH ST.
- Temple Emanu-El
- EAST 63RD ST.
- EAST 60TH ST.
- EAST 57TH ST.
- Museum of Modern Art
- St. Patrick's Cathedral
- Rockefeller Center
- Grand Central Terminal
- New York Public Library
- FIFTH AVENUE
- SIXTH AVENUE

1 Empire State Building (see p. 78) This 1,250-foot (381 m) skyscraper has been captured in such classic films as *King Kong* and *An Affair to Remember*. Walk north on Fifth Avenue and west on 34th Street. Take the B, D, F, or M train at 34th St.–Herald Sq. station to 47th–50th Sts.– Rockefeller Center.

6 Times Square (see pp. 90–91) Once tawdry and unsafe, this bustling, neon-lit area is now among the city's most tourist-friendly spots. Walk to your chosen Broadway theater, whether your taste is for blockbuster musical or edgy drama.

NEW YORK IN A WEEKEND DISTANCE: 4 MILES (6.4 KM) TIME: 8 HOURS SUBWAY START: 34TH ST.–HERALD SQ.

MIDTOWN

Jacob Javits Convention Center

Empire State Building

Morgan Library & Museum

WEST 34TH STREET

EAST 34TH STREET

34th Street–Herald Square

Madison Square Garden

Pennsylvania Station

CHELSEA

WEST 23RD STREET

WEST 28TH STREET

AVENUE

SEVENTH AVENUE

EIGHTH AVENUE

NINTH AVENUE

TENTH AVENUE

ELEVENTH AVE

WEST 34TH STREET

GREENWICH AVENUE

WEST 4TH STREET

AVENUE OF THE AMERICAS

FIFTH AVENUE

MADISON SQUARE PARK

MADISON AVENUE

PARK AVE

LEXINGTON

THIRD

SECOND

EAST 23RD ST.

GRAMERCY PARK

EAST 20TH ST.

UNION SQUARE

N

0 ½ mile

0 1 kilometer

New York in a Weekend

Downtown

Classic sights combine with high fashion.

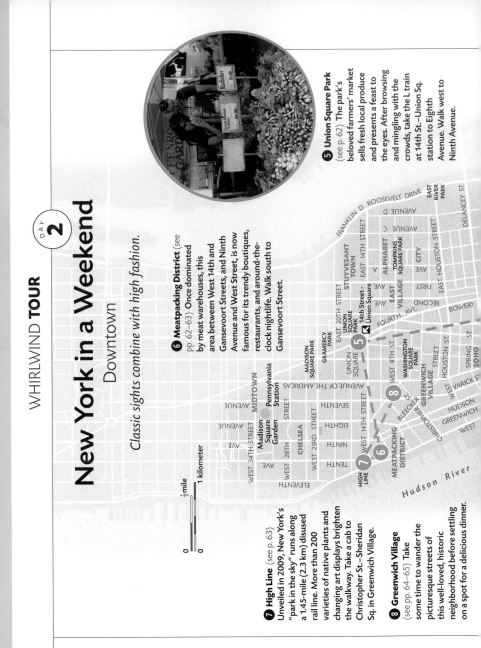

6 Meatpacking District (see pp. 62–63) Once dominated by meat warehouses, this area between West 14th and Gansevoort Streets, and Ninth Avenue and West Street, is now famous for its trendy boutiques, restaurants, and around-the-clock nightlife. Walk south to Gansevoort Street.

5 Union Square Park (see p. 62) The park's beloved farmers' market sells fresh local produce and presents a feast to the eyes. After browsing and mingling with the crowds, take the L train at 14th St.–Union Sq. station to Eighth Avenue. Walk west to Ninth Avenue.

7 High Line (see p. 63) Unveiled in 2009, New York's "park in the sky" runs along a 1.45-mile (2.3 km) disused rail line. More than 200 varieties of native plants and changing art displays brighten the walkway. Take a cab to Christopher St.–Sheridan Sq. in Greenwich Village.

8 Greenwich Village (see pp. 64–65) Take some time to wander the picturesque streets of this well-loved, historic neighborhood before settling on a spot for a delicious dinner.

① Staten Island Ferry (see p. 23) A free, 25-minute ride from the tip of Manhattan guarantees superb views of the Statue of Liberty. On your return, walk northwest to State Street. Turn north on Broadway and right on Wall Street.

② Wall Street (see p. 46) Stroll along Wall Street, among the towering bastions of world finance. Federal Hall, where George Washington was inaugurated, and the New York Stock Exchange are among the area's highlights. Retrace your steps and continue north on Broadway.

③ World Trade Center (see p. 48) Visit the National September 11 Memorial & Museum to learn more about and honor that tragic day. Then, put fear of heights on hold at the top-of-its-class observatory in One World Trade Center, with its spectacular 1,250-foot-high (380 m) views.

④ Chinatown (see p. 49) This vivid area is packed with new sights and tastes. Walk north on Bowery to Canal Street, west to Canal Street station, and take the 6 train to Union Square.

Map labels:
HOLLAND TUNNEL
TRIBECA
CANAL STREET
Canal Street
CHURCH ST
STREET
STREET
STREET
CHAMBERS ST
World Financial Center
World Trade Center Site
BATTERY PARK CITY
Ellis Island
Statue of Liberty
BATTERY PARK
LITTLE ITALY
GRAND ST.
CANAL ST.
LOWER EAST SIDE
MADISON ST.
BOWERY
ROW
Confucius Plaza
CHINA-TOWN ④
BROADWAY
③
PARK
FINANCIAL DISTRICT
FULTON STREET
Civic Center and City Hall
WALL ST.
② N.Y. Stock Exchange
WATER ST.
ELEVATED HIGHWAY
South Street Seaport Historic District
U.S. Customs House
① South Ferry
Staten Island
N

**NEW YORK IN A WEEKEND   DISTANCE: 6.2 MILES (10 KM)
TIME: APPROX. 6 HOURS   SUBWAY START: SOUTH FERRY**

Tips

These major New York sights can be seen in two days. Refer to the cross-references for detailed information elsewhere in the book. Here you'll find information on detours to nearby sights and local cafés and restaurants and suggestions for customizing the tour to suit your own interests.

DAY 1

❷ **Rockefeller Center** (see pp. 92–93) Before or after, detour one block south to ■ DIAMOND ROW (*47th St. between 5th and 6th Aves.*), a world of priceless gems.

❸ **St. Patrick's Cathedral** (see pp. 93–94) Before you go, check out the busy program of ■ FREE CONCERTS

MoMA's The Modern offers French-American cuisine and more than 900 wine selections.

of choir or organ music, and the service schedule. Mass is held several times a day; some are music masses and the 4 p.m. Sunday service is in Spanish.

❹ **Museum of Modern Art** (see pp. 96–97) Combine your visit with fine dining and book in advance for ■ THE MODERN, run by the celebrated restaurateur Thomas Allan, who also runs the two museum cafés. ■ CAFE 2 on the second floor serves panini, pasta, and salads, and has an espresso bar. ■ TERRACE CAFÉ on the fifth floor notches up the sophistication level with wine flights and artisanal cheeses. It has views of the central Sculpture Garden and the skyline, and you can dine on the terrace seasonally.

❺ **Central Park** (see pp. 120–127) Before your visit, make a quick detour to check out the free exhibitions at ■ THE GROLIER CLUB (*47 East 60th St.,* between Madison and Park Aves.), the country's oldest society for lovers of books and the graphic arts.

DAY 2

❶ Staten Island Ferry (*Whitehall Terminal, 1 South St., Subway: 1, R, W to South Ferry; 4, 5 to Bowling Green, siferry .com*) Take a jacket, as the winds can be chilly, even in summertime. You have to debark on arrival at the island and reboard via the waiting room.

❷ Wall Street (see pp. 46–47) While you're in the vicinity, take a rest from the intensely financial milieu and savor the spiritual feel of the Gothic Revival–style ■ **TRINITY CHURCH** (see pp. 47–48).

❹ Chinatown (see p. 49) The city's oldest spot for dim sum is ■ **NOM WAH TEA PARLOR** (*13 Doyers St., near Bowery*), which—refreshingly—hasn't changed much since it opened in 1920. At ■ **TASTY HAND-PULLED NOODLES** (*1 Doyers St., off Chatham Square*), you can feast on hand-stretched or knife-cut noodles—equally delicious—in a bowl of soup. For a restful break after walking through Chinatown, visit the ■ **LIZ CHRISTY COMMUNITY GARDEN** (*corner of Houston St. and Bowery*), the city's first community garden.

CUSTOMIZING **YOUR DAY**

If modern art is not for you, other art options beckon a short $10-15 cab ride away from St. Patrick's Cathedral. The enormous **Metropolitan Museum of Art** (see pp. 112–115) is truly comprehensive. **The Frick Collection** (see p. 106), housed in the former residence of industrialist and art collector Henry Clay Frick, is a smaller, more intimate choice, and even closer.

❼ High Line (see p. 63) Don't miss the amphitheater-like ■ **10TH AVENUE SQUARE**, above the 10th Avenue– 17th Street crossing, with its views of Midtown and the Statue of Liberty.

❽ Greenwich Village (see pp. 64–65) Among the great dining options in the Village is ■ **MINETTA TAVERN** (*113 Macdougal St.*), a clubby, speakeasy-like restaurant famous for its black label burger—a must-order for weekend brunch, or opt for poached eggs atop latkes and smoked salmon. It is part of an empire of fun, late-night spots, with terrific but casual service and big, delicious portions. Or try ■ **PEARL OYSTER BAR** (*18 Cornelia St.*), always packed and lively. The seafood is super-fresh, with lobster rolls and shoestring fries one of the best dishes on the menu.

New York for Fun

Visit the city's top places for views, fashion, and cocktails.

1 Breakfast at Tiffany's (see p. 26) Audrey Hepburn as Holly Golightly was on to something—pastries and diamonds are a perfect start to the day at the Blue Box café. Continue south from 57th Street.

2 Fifth Avenue Shopping (see p. 26) This legendary street is home to the flagship stores of some of fashion's greatest names. Keep strolling to 51st Street.

3 NBC Studios (see p. 26) At Rockefeller Plaza, enjoy a behind-the-scenes peek of your favorite TV show and learn about the history of this major television network. Back on Fifth Avenue, walk down to 34th Street, or take the B, D, F, or M train from Rockefeller Center to 34th St.–Herald Sq.

4 Empire State Building (see pp. 26, 78) At the heart of Manhattan, the landmark skyscraper never fails to enrapture the first-time visitor. Take the B, D, F, or M train from Herald Square to West 4th St.– Washington Sq., or a cab to Bleecker Street.

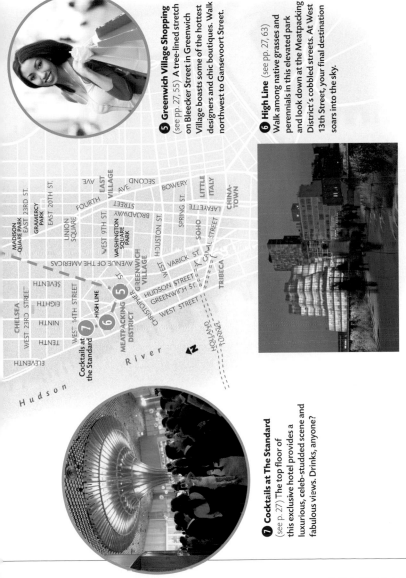

5 Greenwich Village Shopping
(see pp. 27, 55) A tree-lined stretch on Bleecker Street in Greenwich Village boasts some of the hottest designers and chic boutiques. Walk northwest to Gansevoort Street.

6 High Line (see pp. 27, 63) Walk among native grasses and perennials in this elevated park and look down at the Meatpacking District's cobbled streets. At West 13th Street, your final destination soars into the sky.

7 Cocktails at The Standard
(see p. 27) The top floor of this exclusive hotel provides a luxurious, celeb-studded scene and fabulous views. Drinks, anyone?

CHELSEA
WEST 23RD STREET
WEST 14TH STREET
SEVENTH
EIGHTH
NINTH
TENTH
ELEVENTH

MADISON SQUARE PARK
EAST 23RD ST
GRAMERCY PARK
EAST 20TH STREET
UNION SQUARE
FOURTH
EAST VILLAGE
EAST
AVE
SECOND AVE
BOWERY
LAFAYETTE STREET
SPRING ST.
LITTLE ITALY
CHINA-TOWN
SOHO
CANAL STREET
BROADWAY
WEST HOUSTON ST.
WEST 9TH ST.
WASHINGTON SQUARE PARK
AVENUE OF THE AMERICAS
GREENWICH VILLAGE
WEST VARICK ST.
HUDSON STREET
GREENWICH ST.
WEST STREET
CHRISTOPHER ST
TRIBECA
HOLLAND TUNNEL
MEATPACKING DISTRICT
HIGH LINE
Cocktails at the Standard

Hudson River

WHIRLWIND TOURS

NEW YORK FOR FUN DISTANCE: 7.3 MILES (11.7 KM)
TIME: 7 HOURS SUBWAY START: 57TH ST.

Breakfast at Tiffany's

1 Start at the most dreamy of luxury stores: Tiffany & Co., strategically located on legendary Fifth Avenue. First breakfast at Tiffany's Blue Box café, or choose a takeout breakfast from nearby **Sarabeth's** *(40 Central Park South),* then while you savor your pastry, make your imaginary choices from the gem-starred window displays.

Fifth Ave. at 57th St. • tel 212/755-8000 • Subway: F to 57th St. • tiffany.com

Fifth Avenue Shopping

2 Peruse the latest concoctions of the world's top designers along New York's premier shopping strip. Here every shopper can fulfill their haute couture wish list, whether it includes an exquisite suit from **Bergdorf Goodman** *(No. 754),* pearls from **Mikimoto** *(No. 730),* or diamond baubles from **Harry Winston** *(No. 712).*

Below 57th St. • Subway: F to 57th St. • visit5thavenue.com

See how a national television
network operates at Rockefeller
Center's historic NBC Studios.

NBC Studios

3 You can reserve to witness the making of such signature NBC programs as Saturday Night Live. On a guided NBC Studio Tour, you'll see television sets, the broadcast control room, and the studios of Saturday Night Live and more.

30 Rockefeller Plaza • tel 212/664-3700 • $$$$$ tour• Subway: F, D, B to 47th-50th Sts.–Rockefeller Center • nbc.com/tickets

Empire State Building

4 For classic Manhattan views, take the elevator to the 86th or 102nd floor of the city's most elegant building. Sweep the sights through the fixed, high-powered binoculars.

350 Fifth Ave., between 33rd and 34th Sts. • tel 212/736-3100 • Observatory tickets: $$$$$ • Subway: D, F, N,Q, R to 34th St.–Herald Square • esbnyc.com

Greenwich Village Shopping

5 Downtown, tree-lined Bleecker Street combines big-name designer boutiques with a small-town feel. Shop for killer heels and leather accessories at **Il Bisonte** *(No. 381)*, or dip into **Cynthia Rowley** *(No. 394)* and **Intermix** *(No. 365)*. Then sample a friendly Village café, such as **Tea & Sympathy** *(108 Greenwich Ave.)*, a cozy English gem. (See p. 55 for more stylish shopping.)

Between Seventh Ave. and Bank St. • Subway: 1 to Christopher St.–Sheridan Square

High Line

6 This park set at treetop level is a magical place to sit down and sun yourself, or to stroll and gaze down on the New York streets. Beginning in the northwest corner of Greenwich Village, you'll come across flower patches and art displays—all with views of the Hudson River.

Between Gansevoort and West 30th Sts. • tel 212/500-6035 • Subway: A,C, E, L to 14th St.–Eighth Ave. • thehighline.org

Cocktails at The Standard

7 Floor-to-ceiling windows look out over the city from the top of this uber-trendy hotel above the High Line. There's no sign in the lobby to this secret aerie, so just take the elevator to the 18th floor. From hostesses in goddess-style dresses to a magnificent round bar, it's all glam. Sip a delicious, if pricey, cocktail and watch the boats from a white leather sofa facing the Hudson River. From two cozy nooks on the south side, you can see Wall Street and the Statue of Liberty. Visit the bathroom before you leave; you'll never forget it!

848 Washington St. at 13th St. • tel 212/645-4646 • Subway: A, C, E, L to 14th St.–Eighth Ave. • standardhotels.com

GOOD **EATS**

■ **ALIDORO**
Pop into this popular Midtown outpost for a classic Italian cheesesteak sandwich with sautéed mushrooms, provolone, and truffle cream. **30 Rockefeller Plaza, tel 646/688-3596, $**

■ **BUVETTE**
Mirroring a cozy Parisian café, Buvette replicates authentic French style, from bistro-aproned servers to a seasonal menu featuring escargot. **42 Grove St., tel 212/255-3590, $$**

■ **FOOD GALLERY 32**
Near the Empire State Building, this Korean food court houses independent stalls selling tasty noodles, rice dishes, soups, and stews. **11 West 32nd St., $**

WHIRLWIND TOURS

New York in a Weekend with Kids

Downtown

After playing outdoors, let the imagination run wild at the downtown museums.

3 The Tenement Museum (see pp. 30–31) Beginning in 1863, the modest apartment building at 97 Orchard Street was home to nearly 7,000 immigrants. Explore the lives of residents through tours, digital exhibits, and more. Turn west on Delancey Street, then Spring Street, and head north on Broadway.

4 Museum of Ice Cream (see p. 31) Who could deny their kids an obligatory stop at this fun, all-pink museum with multi-sensory installations, including a sprinkle pool? Return to Spring Street and follow it west.

5 New York City Fire Museum (see p. 31) In a renovated 1904 firehouse, this museum adds historical heft to the hip SoHo area. It has one of the nation's most important collections of fire-related art and artifacts, some dating back to the 18th century, with plenty of hands-on fun.

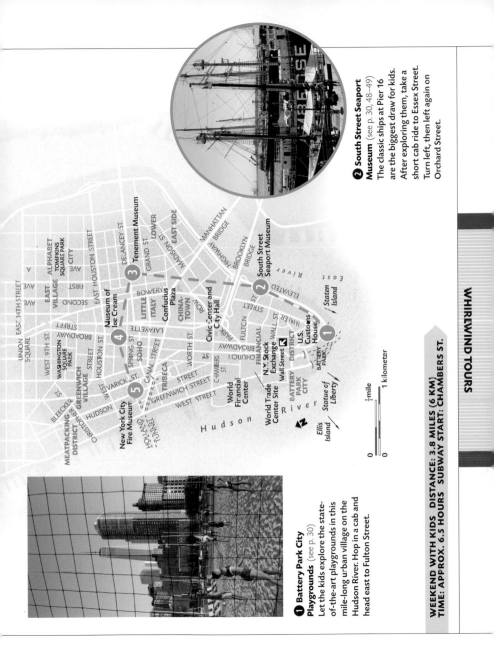

① Battery Park City Playgrounds (see p. 30)
Let the kids explore the state-of-the-art playgrounds in this mile-long urban village on the Hudson River. Hop in a cab and head east to Fulton Street.

② South Street Seaport Museum (see p. 30, 48–49)
The classic ships at Pier 16 are the biggest draw for kids. After exploring them, take a short cab ride to Essex Street. Turn left, then left again on Orchard Street.

WEEKEND WITH KIDS DISTANCE: 3.8 MILES (6 KM)
TIME: APPROX. 6.5 HOURS SUBWAY START: CHAMBERS ST.

WHIRLWIND TOURS

Map labels:
UNION SQUARE
EAST 14TH STREET
WEST 9TH ST.
WASHINGTON SQUARE PARK
BROADWAY
BLEECKER ST.
GREENWICH VILLAGE
MEATPACKING DISTRICT
CHRISTOPHER ST.
HUDSON ST.
EAST HOUSTON STREET
WEST HOUSTON STREET
SECOND
FIRST
AVE
A
ALPHABET CITY
TOMPKINS SQUARE PARK
EAST VILLAGE
DELANCEY ST.
GRAND ST.
LOWER EAST SIDE
MADISON ST.
MANHATTAN BRIDGE
③ Tenement Museum
④ Museum of Ice Cream
SPRING ST.
SOHO
LAFAYETTE STREET
LITTLE ITALY
BOWERY
Confucius Plaza
CHINA-TOWN
BROOKLYN BRIDGE
VARICK ST.
CANAL STREET
TRIBECA
GREENWICH STREET
WORTH ST.
CHAMBERS ST.
Civic Center and City Hall
PARK ROW
FULTON ST.
② South Street Seaport Museum
PIER 16
STREET ELEVATED
East River
⑤ New York City Fire Museum
HOLLAND TUNNEL
WEST STREET
World Financial Center
World Trade Center Site
BATTERY PARK CITY
CHURCH ST.
BROADWAY
N.Y. Stock Exchange
Wall Street
FINANCIAL DISTRICT
WALL STREET
U.S. Customs House
① Battery Park
Staten Island
Statue of Liberty
Ellis Island
Hudson River

½ mile
1 kilometer
0
0

Battery Park City Playgrounds

Battery Park City is a waterfront neighborhood that stretches from Chambers Street in the north to Battery Park in the south along the Hudson River. Not only does it guarantee some of the most stunning views in New York, it also houses a handful of imaginative playgrounds and open spaces. Start at the largest and northernmost park, **Rockefeller,** which is decked out with sand and water equipment and contains separate areas for older and younger kids. Then stroll south along the esplanade, checking out glimpses of the **Statue of Liberty** (see pp. 50–51) and the New Jersey shoreline. Make another stop at **Teardrop Park,** a smaller, leafy playground built directly into the craggy hillside.

North end of Battery Park City, west of River Terrace • tel 212/267-9700 • 1, 2, 3, A, C to Chambers St. • nycgovparks.org

GOOD **EATS**

■ **CHARLIE BIRD**
Cavatelli with sausage, light pastas, and a raw oyster bar explain its popularity. **King St., tel 212/235-7133, $$**

■ **FAMOUS BEN'S PIZZA**
Another SoHo stop-off is especially famous for its wide variety of pizza toppings. **177 Spring St.,tel 212 966 4494, $**

■ **VANESSA'S DUMPLING HOUSE**
Head to City Acres Market for handmade dumplings, buns, noodles, and sesame pancakes. **70 Pine St., tel 917262-4531 ext. 5, $-$$, vanessas.com**

■ **KATZ'S DELICATESSEN**
Drop by the ultimate Lower East Side deli for a sandwich, hot dog with fries, or knish. Portions are generous, so you could split one meal between two kids. **205 East Houston St., tel 212/254-2246, $**

South Street Seaport Museum

If your kids love ships and history, head to the South Street Seaport Museum, downtown on the East River. Indoors, landlubbers can pore over scale models of the *Titanic* and the Cunard Line's *Queen Mary,* and memorabilia from the days of luxury liners. Would-be seafarers should make for Pier 16, part of the museum where historic ships are moored. Climb aboard the 1907 *Ambrose* **lightship** or explore the three-masted *Wavertree* (1885), one of the largest—and last—iron-hulled sailing vessels ever built.

12 Fulton St. • tel 212/748-8600 • Closed Mon. and Tue. • $$ for Ships Only tour • Subway: 2, 3, 4, 5, A, C to Fulton St. • seany.org

Tenement Museum

This museum is the real thing—a fully refurbished tenement building where many immigrant families lived. At the Visitor Center on 103 Orchard Street book one of the tenement apartment tours that introduce visitors to the lives of various families, from 19th–century Chinese immigrants to holocaust survivors and Puerto Rican immigrants of the 1950s. Neighborhood Walking Tours explore the varied histories of migration over centuries while exploring often-forgotten places of the Lower East Side.

103 Orchard St. • tel 877/975-3786 • Closed Jan. 1, Thanksgiving, and Dec. 25 • $$$$$ guided tour • Subway: F, J to Essex –Delancey Sts. • tenement.org

Kids participate in a class in the Fine Art Studio at the Children's Museum of the Arts.

Museum of Ice Cream

4 Kids and adults alike can enjoy the scoop on ice cream and its history in this interactive fantasy wonderland, with 13 fun, multi-sensory art installations, including a 3D movie, a Celestial Subway, and a rainbow tunnel made of sprinkles. You can even splash around in a sprinkle pool filled with more than one hundred million non-edible giant sprinkles. Entry includes ice cream tastings and signature treats, and a café and shop sells milkshakes and specialty sundaes.

558 Broadway • Closed holidays • $$$$$ • Subway: N, Q, R & W to Prince St.; C, E to Spring St. • museumoficecream.com

New York City Fire Museum

5 In this revamped beaux arts firehouse in SoHo, kids can try on gear and see hand-pumped engines, four-wheel hose reels, a horse-drawn 1901 steam engine, and motorized vehicles of the 1920s. Historic tools on display include leather fire buckets, alarm boxes, and speaking trumpets. Actual firefighters are often present to instill fire safety tips and answer questions.

278 Spring St., between Varick and Hudson Sts. • tel 212/691-1303 • Closed Mon. and Tues., major holidays • $$ • Subway: C, E to Spring St. or 1 to Houston St. • nycfiremuseum.org

New York in a Weekend with Kids

The best views of the city set the scene for adventures in science and nature.

⑤ American Museum of Natural History (see pp. 35, 140–141) Founded in 1869, this museum continues to meet its lofty ambitions to serve as a guide to the universe, the natural world, and human culture. Travel to the depths of the ocean and into the infinity of space before dinner. Walk east on West 77th St. to Central Park.

⑥ The Lake (see p. 35) Rent a rowboat or gondola at Loeb Boathouse and spend a peaceful hour or two spotting herons, egrets, waterfowl, and other birds.

WEST 96TH ST.

UPPER WEST SIDE

WEST 86TH STREET

Children's Museum of Manhattan

CENTRAL PARK WEST

Jacqueline Kennedy Onassis Reservoir

BROADWAY AVE
AVE

④

RIVERSIDE DRIVE

END

American Museum of Natural History

⑤

⑥ The Lake

CENTRAL

WEST 76TH ST.

HENRY HUDSON PARKWAY

WEST 72ND BUS

Whitney Museum of American Art

EAST 72ND ST.

AVE

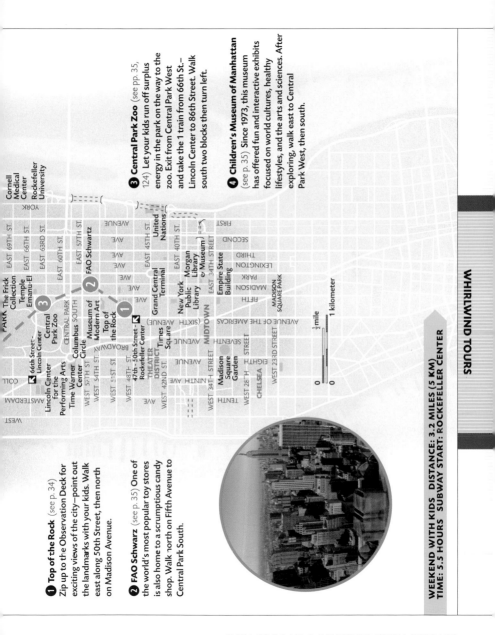

① Top of the Rock (see p. 34)
Zip up to the Observation Deck for exciting views of the city—point out the landmarks with your kids. Walk east along 50th Street, then north on Madison Avenue.

② FAO Schwarz (see p. 35) One of the world's most popular toy stores is also home to a scrumptious candy shop. Walk north on Fifth Avenue to Central Park South.

③ Central Park Zoo (see pp. 35, 124) Let your kids run off surplus energy in the park on the way to the zoo. Exit from Central Park West and take the 1 train from 66th St.–Lincoln Center to 86th Street. Walk south two blocks then turn left.

④ Children's Museum of Manhattan (see p. 35) Since 1973, this museum has offered fun and interactive exhibits focused on world cultures, healthy lifestyles, and the arts and sciences. After exploring, walk east to Central Park West, then south.

WHIRLWIND TOURS

WEEKEND WITH KIDS DISTANCE: 3.2 MILES (5 KM)
TIME: 5.5 HOURS SUBWAY START: ROCKEFELLER CENTER

Top of the Rock

1 Towering above bustling Midtown, the Top of the Rock observation deck occupies floors 67, 69, and 70 of Rockefeller Center. An elevator whisks you up to the 360-degree views, which you can see from glass-covered terraces, or outside at the highest level, 850 feet (260 m) above ground. On a clear day, it's easy to spot the **Statue of Liberty.** Floor-to-ceiling windows make it easy even for little kids to see all around, and kids under six get in free.

30 Rockefeller Plaza • tel 212/698-2000 • $$$$$ • Subway: F, D to 47th-50th Sts.– Rockefeller Center • topoftherocknyc.com

FAO Schwarz

2 More than just the oldest toy store in the United States, FAO Schwarz is packed with games, gifts, and playthings from classic dolls to modern slot cars. It is also the home of the giant piano made famous in the Tom Hanks movie *Big*.

30 Rockefeller Plaza • tel 800/326-8638 • Closed major holidays • Subway: B, D, F, M to 47-5o Sts./Rockefeller Center • faoschwarz.com

Central Park Zoo

3 Kids will love saying "Hi" to the animals that live in the Central Park Zoo, enormous grizzly bears and barking sea lions being favorites. Younger ones can get close to smaller animals at the **Tisch Children's Zoo,** a short walk from the main site, where they can pet goats, sheep, and pigs.

Fifth Ave. and 64th St.• tel 212/439-6500 • $$$$ • Subway: N, Q, R to Fifth Ave./59th St. • centralparkzoo.com

A doorman dressed as a toy soldier stands outside the FAO Schwarz flagship store.

Children's Museum of Manhattan

 The museum is organized according to kids' ages. Under-fours will enjoy

educational fun with **PlayWorks** on the third floor. School-age kids should check out the first floor's changing exhibits and performances. The museum often features an exhibit with a lovable character, such as **Adventures with Dora and Diego.** Older kids will appreciate the fourth-floor displays, which explore topics ranging from ancient Greece to Dr. Seuss.

212 West 83rd St. between Broadway and Amsterdam Ave. • tel 212/721-1223 • Closed Mon., Jan. 1, Thanksgiving, and Dec. 25 • $$ • Subway: 1 to 79th or 86th Sts. or B, C to 81st St. • cmom.org

American Museum of Natural History

5 Don't miss the giant blue whale in the **Milstein Family Hall of Ocean Life,** life-size copies of a fossilized **prehistoric** *Barosaurus* mother and baby, and the **Rose Center for Earth and Space,** where the **Hayden Planetarium Space Show** delves into the origins of the universe. Advance ticketing is recommended and can be done online or on the phone.

Central Park West at 79th St. • tel 212/769-5100 • $$$$$ • Closed Thanksgiving and Dec. 25 • Subway: B, C to 81st.–Museum of Natural History • amnh.org

The Lake

6 In 1857, designers Frederick Law Olmsted and Calvert Vaux turned an untamed swamp into the picturesque 20-acre (8 ha) Central Park Lake. It draws waterfowl and is an excellent location for birdwatching while strolling or from a boat, available for rent at the Loeb Boathouse.

West Dr. & Terrace Dr. • tel 212/310-6600 • Subway: B, C to Central Park West–72nd St. • centralpark.com

GOOD **EATS**

■ **ANGELO'S PIZZERIA**
When near Central Park Zoo, treat the kids to scrumptious pizza heaped with your choice of toppings. Save room for chocolate mousse cake or gelato. **117 West 57th St., tel 212/333-4333. $**

■ **BARNEY GREENGRASS**
An NYC institution since 1908, this beloved spot serves up classic deli fare and is famous for its smoked and cured fish. **541 Amsterdam Ave., tel 212/724-4707, $$**

PART 2

New York's Neighborhoods

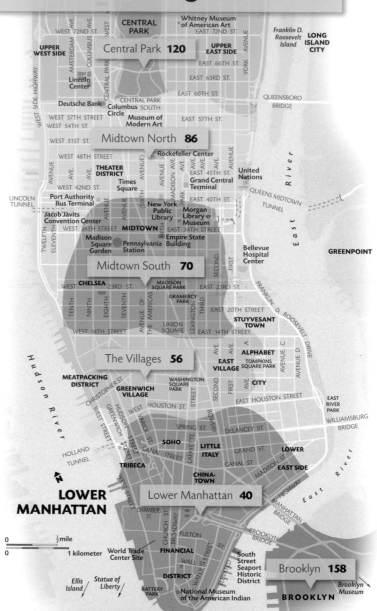

New York's Neighborhoods

CENTRAL PARK

Whitney Museum of American Art

EAST 72ND ST.

WEST 72ND ST.

Franklin D. Roosevelt Island

LONG ISLAND CITY

UPPER WEST SIDE

Central Park **120**

UPPER EAST SIDE

EAST 66TH ST.

EAST 63RD ST.

Lincoln Center

EAST 60TH ST.

QUEENSBORO BRIDGE

Deutsche Bank

CENTRAL PARK SOUTH

Columbus Circle

Museum of Modern Art

EAST 57TH ST.

WEST 57TH STREET

WEST 54TH ST.

Midtown North **86**

WEST 51ST ST.

WEST 48TH STREET

Rockefeller Center

THEATER DISTRICT

EAST 45TH ST.

United Nations

Times Square

Grand Central Terminal

WEST 42ND ST.

EAST 40TH ST.

QUEENS MIDTOWN TUNNEL

LINCOLN TUNNEL

Port Authority Bus Terminal

New York Public Library

Morgan Library & Museum

Jacob Javits Convention Center

WEST 34TH STREET

MIDTOWN

EAST 34TH STREET

Madison Square Garden

Pennsylvania Station

Empire State Building

Bellevue Hospital Center

GREENPOINT

Midtown South **70**

CHELSEA

23RD ST.

MADISON SQUARE PARK

EAST 23RD ST.

GRAMERCY PARK

EAST 20TH STREET

STUYVESANT TOWN

UNION SQUARE

WEST 14TH STREET

EAST 14TH STREET

The Villages **56**

ALPHABET

TOMPKINS SQUARE PARK

MEATPACKING DISTRICT

WASHINGTON SQUARE PARK

EAST VILLAGE

CITY

GREENWICH VILLAGE

EAST HOUSTON STREET

EAST RIVER PARK

HOUSTON ST.

WILLIAMSBURG BRIDGE

HOLLAND TUNNEL

SPRING ST.

DELANCEY ST.

SOHO

LITTLE ITALY

GRAND ST.

LOWER EAST SIDE

TRIBECA

CANAL ST.

CHINA-TOWN

LOWER MANHATTAN

Lower Manhattan **40**

CHAMBERS ST.

FULTON ST.

BROOKLYN BRIDGE

½ mile

1 kilometer

World Trade Center Site

FINANCIAL

WALL ST.

South Street Seaport Historic District

Brooklyn **158**

Ellis Island

Statue of Liberty

DISTRICT

BATTERY PARK

National Museum of the American Indian

Brooklyn Museum

BROOKLYN

Hudson River

East River

FRANKLIN D. ROOSEVELT DRIVE

MANHATTAN BRIDGE

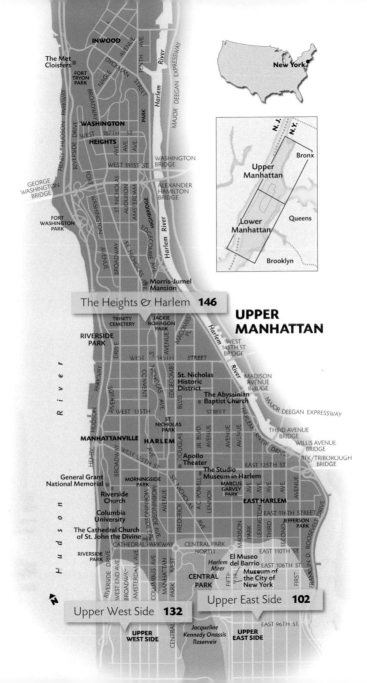

INWOOD

The Met
Cloisters

FORT
TRYON
PARK

WASHINGTON
HEIGHTS

WEST 187TH ST

WEST 181ST ST

WASHINGTON
BRIDGE

GEORGE
WASHINGTON
BRIDGE

ALEXANDER
HAMILTON
BRIDGE

FORT
WASHINGTON
PARK

HIGHBRIDGE

Harlem River

Morris-Jumel
Mansion

The Heights & Harlem 146

TRINITY
CEMETERY

JACKIE
ROBINSON
PARK

RIVERSIDE
PARK

WEST 145TH STREET

WEST 145TH ST
BRIDGE

MADISON
AVENUE
BRIDGE

St. Nicholas
Historic
District

The Abyssinian
Baptist Church

WEST 135TH   STREET

ST.
NICHOLAS
PARK

MANHATTANVILLE

HARLEM

WEST 125TH ST

MAJOR DEEGAN EXPRESSWAY

THIRD AVENUE
BRIDGE

WILLIS AVENUE
BRIDGE

RFK/TRIBOROUGH
BRIDGE

Apollo
Theater

The Studio
Museum in Harlem

MARCUS
GARVEY
PARK

EAST 125TH ST

General Grant
National Memorial

MORNINGSIDE
PARK

Riverside
Church

Columbia
University

The Cathedral Church
of St. John the Divine

CATHEDRAL PARKWAY

CENTRAL PARK
NORTH

EAST HARLEM

EAST 116TH STREET

JEFFERSON
PARK

EAST 110TH ST

RIVERSIDE
PARK

El Museo
del Barrio

Harlem
Meer

Museum of
the City of
New York

EAST 106TH ST

Upper East Side 102

CENTRAL
PARK

Jacqueline
Kennedy Onassis
Reservoir

Upper West Side 132

UPPER
WEST SIDE

UPPER
EAST SIDE

EAST 96TH ST.

**UPPER
MANHATTAN**

New York

N.J.
N.Y.

Upper
Manhattan

Bronx

Lower
Manhattan

Queens

Brooklyn

Lower Manhattan

Lower Manhattan technically constitutes everything below Houston Street and between the Hudson and East Rivers, but Tribeca and SoHo in the upper-west corner form artsy enclaves all their own. What really defines the area is the historic role it played in the founding of New York City and in turning it into a commercial power. At the tip of Manhattan, the Dutch purchased the island from the local Lenape people in 1626, and the city subsequently came under British control in 1664. Later, in 1785, New York became the first capital of the new nation following the Revolutionary War. The Statue of Liberty and Ellis Island in New York Harbor give some perspective on Manhattan as an island and offer a small reminder of New York's maritime history. But the most poignant effect Lower Manhattan has on the imagination may be as the site of the World Trade Center attacks of September 11, 2001. The rebuilding of the area is testament to the enduring spirit with which Lower Manhattan was settled centuries ago.

◀ **The Statue of Liberty arrived in New York Harbor in 1886, in 350 pieces. It was reassembled and dedicated in October of that year.**

Lower Manhattan

The packed neighborhoods of Lower Manhattan are diverse, merging immigrant culture with the bustle of Wall Street.

⑤ Fraunces Tavern (see pp. 45–46) The site of Washington's farewell address to the Continental Army in 1783 is a museum of pre-Revolutionary artifacts. Continue on Pearl Street and turn left onto Wall Street.

④ National Museum of the American Indian (see pp. 44–45) Located in the grand rotunda of the 1907 Custom House, the museum presents Native American culture in rotating exhibitions. Turn right onto State Street, left onto Bridge Street, and cross to Pearl Street.

③ Ellis Island (see p. 44) Visit the gateway to a new world for millions of immigrants. Return by ferry to Castle Clinton and cross the park to Bowling Green.

② Statue of Liberty National Monument (see pp. 50–51) Take the ferry to Liberty Island, where France's gift is even more impressive up close— a museum in the statue's base tells the story. Continue by ferry to Ellis Island.

① Battery Park (see p. 44) Start at one of New York's oldest public spaces. Battery Park is the departure point for ferries to the Statue of Liberty and Ellis Island. Get tickets at Castle Clinton National Monument, the fort built for the War of 1812.

LOWER MANHATTAN   DISTANCE: 7 MILES (11 KM)
TIME: APPROX. 8 HOURS   SUBWAY START: BOWLING GREEN

11 Chinatown (see p. 49) Peruse embroidered silk goods, exotic teas, and cheap watches; taste dumplings, noodles, and Peking duck to complete the day.

10 South Street Seaport Historic District (see pp. 48–49) Once America's center of commerce, the area still has tall ships in the harbor and offers plenty of great options for shopping, eating, and entertainment. Take the subway (J train) from Fulton Street to Canal Street at Centre Street.

9 World Trade Center (see p. 48) Visit the site and museum built to commemorate the tragedy on September 11, 2001. Turn right on Broadway and left on Fulton Street.

8 Trinity Church (see pp. 47–48) With a museum, concerts, church services, and a graveyard, Trinity has been a place for contemplation for more than 300 years. Turn left up Trinity Place; Vesey Street is six blocks up on the left.

7 Federal Hall National Memorial (see p. 47) Considered the birthplace of the U.S. government, this is where George Washington took the oath of office as the first president of a new nation. Walk along Wall Street to Broadway.

6 Wall Street (see p. 46) The center of the Financial District has a distinctly European feel with its crowded narrow streets—no surprise, since the Dutch settled the Wall Street area in the 1600s. Federal Hall is two blocks along on the right.

Battery Park

 Dutch settlers landed here in 1623, erecting a battery of cannons to defend the pocket of land they called New Amsterdam. Today, gardens, sculptures, memorials, monuments, and recreation areas fill the 25 acres (10 ha) of downtown's largest public space. Enjoy waterfront views of the Statue of Liberty (see pp. 50–51), tugboats, barges, and sailboats. The park is also home to **Castle Clinton National Monument** *(tel 212/344-7220, closed Dec. nps.gov/cacl),* a fort built to defend against a British invasion in 1812. It served as an immigration center before Ellis Island opened and now holds displays of historic Manhattan.

State St. and Battery Pl. • tel 212/344-3491 • Subway: 4 or 5 to Bowling Green or 1 to South Ferry • thebattery.org

SAVVY **TRAVELER**

A pedestrian paradise, the esplanade along the Hudson River runs the length of residential Battery Park City (Battery Park north to Stuyvesant High School). Transformed from urban scrub into a series of plazas, parks, and gardens, it has benches, picnic tables, and a path for strolling and jogging.

Statue of Liberty National Monument

 See pp. 50–51.

Liberty Island, New York Harbor • tel 212/363-3200 • Closed Dec. 25 • Ferry from Castle Clinton National Monument in Battery Park • Ferry cost includes admission to the monument: $$$$$ • nps.gov/stli

Ellis Island

See pp. 50–51.

Ellis Island, New York Harbor • tel 212/363-3200 • Closed Dec. 25 • Ferry from Castle Clinton National Monument in Battery Park • Ferry cost includes admission to the island and its sites: $$$$$ • nps.gov/elis

National Museum of the American Indian

Part of the Smithsonian Institution (an adjunct opened in Washington, D.C., in 2004), this branch resides in the George Gustav Heye Center, which occupies two floors of the 1907 beaux arts **Alexander Hamilton U.S. Custom House** at the

The National Museum of the American Indian has an archive of some 324,000 photographs.

foot of Broadway. Nearby Bowling Green is reputedly where the
Dutch made a deal for Manhattan Island with the Native American
inhabitants. Exhibits of literature, language, history, and the arts of
American Indians are displayed in the splendid, elliptical **Rotunda,**
lit by a 140-ton (127 tonne) glass skylight.

1 Bowling Green • tel 212/514-3700 • Closed Dec. 25 • Subway: 4 or 5 to Bowling
Green • nmai.si.edu

Fraunces Tavern

5 One of Manhattan's oldest buildings, this tavern was, by the
1760s, a popular meeting place for patriots, known as the
Sons of Liberty. Here, in 1783, George Washington bade farewell
to officers of the Continental Army. Today the site is a museum
complex of four 19th-century buildings, plus the tavern, which was
reconstructed in 1907. In addition to galleries of period paintings

and re-creations of post-Revolutionary rooms that were once government offices, the museum's highlights include more than 200 flags and a lock of George Washington's hair (reddish) and one of his false teeth—evidence that the ardent patriot, general, and first U.S. president was also a normal human being. The rustic Fraunces Tavern basement bar and restaurant, is a good place for a pint of craft beer and shepherd's pie or New England clam chowder. The huge selection of draught brews includes Oyster Stout (sweet and salty) made with fresh oysters simmered in the brew tank until they open up.

54 Pearl St., off Broad St. • tel 212/425-1778 • Closed Mon., Tues., and major public holidays • $$ • Subway: R to Whitehall St. • frauncestavernmuseum.org

Wall Street

6 Pedestrianized since 9/11, Wall Street is home to the NASDAQ Stock Market and the New York Stock Exchange. Feel the pulse as office workers and stockbrokers buzz around, wheeling and dealing on their cell phones, even as they grab a quick lunch from food carts. The days of the wooden stockade built along this route by the governor Peter Stuyvesant to protect the new Dutch settlement, and for which the street is named, are long gone, but nowhere else in Manhattan is so replete with so much history as the Financial District. Don't miss **Stone Street,** full of Dutch revival architecture; and the **New York Stock Exchange** (*corner of Broad and Wall Streets*), with its landmark façade; and the iconic 7,000-pound (3,175 kg), bronze **Charging Bull** sculpture (*Bowling Green Park, on Broadway and Morris St.*) by Arturo Di Modica. An hour-long, reservation-only tour at the **Federal Reserve Bank of New York** (*33 Liberty St., tel 212/720-6130, closed weekends and bank holidays, newyorkfed.org*) includes a peek into the gold vault and entry to the bank's museum, where visitors can see money from all over the world.

Between Broadway and Water St. • Subway: 2, 3, 4, 5 to Wall St. or J, Z to Broad St.

Federal Hall National Memorial

7 Federal Hall is all about George Washington and "firsts." The bronze statue on the front steps marks the spot where Washington was inaugurated as president in 1789. This was the first capitol building of the new nation, where the first U.S. Congress met, and it was also the original City Hall of New York. The current building—an early example of Greek Revival architecture—was finished in 1842. Inside, visitors can see the Bible that Washington used for his oath of office, the railing against which he leaned, and the floor upon which he walked. Reproductions of colonial documents and currency are available in the gift shop. The broad steps outside offer a great view of the narrow historic streets of the nation's first capital city and of the frantic pace of business today.

26 Wall St. • tel 212/825-6990 • Closed Sat., Sun., and major holidays • Subway: 2, 3, 4, 5 to Wall St. or J, Z to Broad St. • nps.gov/feha

Trinity Church

8 This historic church was founded by Anglicans in 1697. Destroyed twice (by fire in 1776 and following heavy snow in 1839), the current church—built in the Gothic Revival style—dates from 1846. You enter through bronze doors sculpted with Biblical scenes similar to those on the Baptistry in Florence, Italy. Inside, the vaulted ceiling opens up the narrow space to a stained-glass wall above the altar. Prominent members of the congregation included Federalist Alexander Hamilton, who is buried in the churchyard. George Washington worshiped at nearby **St. Paul's Chapel** *(Broadway and Fulton St., trinitywallstreet.org/visit/st-pauls-chapel)*, the only original colonial-era church in Manhattan. In spring and fall at Trinity, Thursday concerts *(1 p.m.)* by critically acclaimed musicians provide

The soaring interior of Trinity Church displays many neo-Gothic elements: pointed arches, rib vaulting, and, above the altar, a brilliant stained-glass window.

LOWER MANHATTAN

GOOD **EATS**

■ JOE'S SHANGHAI
Try this Chinatown restaurant for soup dumplings, sesame chicken, or Szechuan–style string beans. **46 Bowery, tel 212/233-8888, $**

■ MARC FORGIONE
Also in Tribeca, chef Marc "Forge" Forgione presents New American dishes in a former butter warehouse. **134 Reade St., tel 212/941-9401, $$$$$**

■ SHAKE SHACK
There's no better place in Battery Park City to feast on delicious burgers, fries, and ice cream. **215 Murray St., tel 646/545-4600, $**

an opportunity to rest and revive. Visitors may attend daily church services or take self-guided tours. But contrary to the 2004 movie *National Treasure,* you will find no elevator shaft to a secret room under the church.

Broadway at Wall St. • tel 212/602-0800 • Subway: 2, 3, 4, 5 to Wall St. or J, Z to Broad St. • trinitywallstreet.org

World Trade Center

9 A visit to the newly designed World Trade Center promises a moving experience—not only because of the tragedy it commemorates, but also because it captures the strength of the human spirit to rebuild. The site—16 acres (6.5 ha) in all—includes five sleek skyscrapers as well as the **9/11 Memorial and Museum,** which provides an in-depth look at the events of September 11. Defining the memorial plaza are two massive pools set within the footprints of the original Twin Towers. Cap off the visit at **One World Observatory,** the 1,250-foot-high (381 m) observation deck on the 100th floor of One World Trade Center. Ticket holders also enjoy access to three dining options on the 101st floor.

120 Liberty St. • $$$$$ (tickets include admission to memorial plaza) • Subway: 2, 3, 4, 5, A, C, J, or Z to Fulton St. • officialworldtradecenter.com

South Street Seaport Historic District

10 Encompassing 11 square blocks around South and Fulton Streets, this district honors New York's maritime history. The **South Street Seaport Museum** *(12 Fulton St., tel 212/748-8600, closed Mon. and Tues., $$$, southstreetseaportmuseum.org)* tells the story of New York as a great world port. The collection includes scrimshaw, more than 1,000 ship models, and one of the best collections of ocean liner memorabilia and ephemera in the

Visitors at the One World Observatory at the One World Trade Center.

country. The real draw is the collection of restored, historic ships at Piers 15 and 16 that include sail- and steam-powered vessels. You can even take harbor tours *(May–Oct., tel 212/619-6900, manhattanbysail. com, $$$$$)* aboard the gaff-rigged schooner *Clipper City.*

Subway: 2, 3, 4, 5, A, C, J, Z to Fulton St. • southstreetseaport.com

Chinatown

If you have time, explore Chinatown's heart. Visit the **Museum of Chinese in America** *(215 Centre St., tel 212/619-4785, $$$, closed Mon.-Fri., Sun., mocanyc.org)*, where short films on Chinese Americans are shown. On Mott Street, visit **Ten Ren** *(No. 75)* to learn about tea and **Chai Spot** *(No. 156)* for tastings. (See p. 23 for other food options.)

Mott and Pell Streets below Canal St. • Subway: N, R, Q, J, Z to Canal St. • chinatown -online.com

Statue of Liberty & Ellis Island

*On a tiny island in New York Harbor many new arrivals
became Americans, both in their hearts and by law.*

A fresh wave of immigrants disembarks at Ellis Island circa 1915.

For the more than 12 million immigrants who crossed the Atlantic between
1892 and 1954, the first glimpse of their new home was a 165-foot (50 m)
copper woman, green from oxidation and holding a torch of liberty. For many,
the experience triggered abundant feelings of joy and hope. Their first steps
on American soil took place just next door on Ellis Island, where they were
checked and registered. Today, the descendants of these immigrants account
for nearly half of the current population of the United States.

LOWER MANHATTAN

■ STATUE OF LIBERTY

Since 1886, this statue, with broken shackles at her feet and a tablet with the date of independence in her hand, has been an inspiration for Americans. A visit includes the **observation deck** and a **museum** in the pedestal. Here you learn the story of sculptor Frédéric-Auguste Bartholdi's creation, which was built with money donated by the French public and shipped across the Atlantic. Don't miss the famous lines from the poem by Emma Lazarus etched on the pedestal: "Give me your tired, your poor, / Your huddled masses yearning to breathe free."

Book months in advance for the highest possible access, to the **crown**, and take your ticket to the Information Booth before the security screening. Climbing the 354 spiraling steps is hard work, but if the exercise doesn't take your breath away, the views will.

■ ELLIS ISLAND

Greeted by stacks of luggage and photos, visitors to the **museum,** which is housed in the old immigration building of 1900, will immediately get a feel for what life was like for the new

arrivals. On January 1, 1892, 15-year-old Annie Moore from Ireland was the first immigrant to be inspected and have her details recorded. Millions followed from all over Europe, and exhibits outline the motives behind their journeys, from persecution and pogroms to lack of work. Artifacts, photographs, interactive exhibits, and oral histories convey the toll of travel and the difficult conditions that immigrants faced when they arrived.

At the **American Family Immigration History Center,** visitors can locate names of relatives at computer stations, or look up noted arrivals such as Albert Einstein. His details read: Landed April 2, 1921, Swiss ethnicity, resided in Berlin, left from Holland on *The Rotterdam*. A printout souvenir (suitable for framing) includes this kind of information and a photo of the ship.

LOWER MANHATTAN

Liberty Island and Ellis Island, New York Harbor • tel 212/363-3200 • Closed Dec. 25 • Ferry from Castle Clinton National Monument in Battery Park • Ferry cost includes admission to the monument: $$$ • nps.gov/stli • nps.gov/elis

A City of Immigrants

It would be impossible to imagine New York without its dynamic immigrant populations, visible, among other places, in the famous Lower Manhattan enclaves of Little Italy and Chinatown. Indeed, every group that has settled here, such as the Italian stonemasons and Eastern European tailors of the 19th century, has added to America's cultural heritage—while the city's diversity and the pace of immigration continue to increase.

Many immigrants lived in cramped Lower East Side tenements, one of which—97 Orchard Street—is now a museum (above). Chinese New Year sees a dragon parade dance through Chinatown's main streets (opposite).

Cosmopolitan Origins

More than 36 percent of New York's population is foreign-born, and more than 800 different languages are spoken, making the city the most linguistically diverse in the world. The first arrivals in the Dutch-owned port town of New Amsterdam in the first half of the 17th century were Danish, English, Flemish, French, German, Irish, Italian, and Norwegian settlers. Many more followed, and by the early 19th century, New York was firmly established as the center of trade and opportunity in the New World. Political upheaval in Europe brought further influxes of immigrants. Between 1892 and 1954, more than 12 million arrivals passed through the Ellis Island immigrant inspection center (see pp. 50–51).

Melting Pot

The familiar "melting pot" term came from a 1908 play of the same name by the Anglo-Jewish activist and writer, Israel Zangwill. The term is somewhat misleading when considering New York, however.

The different ethnic groups that came to the city in the 19th and early 20th centuries did not meld, but clustered in neighborhoods that preserved their language, culture, food, and customs. Many lived in dangerously overcrowded tenements.

Harlem was a refuge for African Americans after the Civil War, while East Harlem, an Italian neighborhood until the 1950s, has since been transformed into a vibrant Latino enclave. There are hundreds more such pockets, some highly specific, where the wanderer can find food, conversation, literature, and people from every corner of the world. They include Little Senegal on 116th Street, where many people originate from French West Africa, and Little Odessa in Brighton Beach, a tiny fragment of Russia in Brooklyn.

ETHNIC **MUSEUMS**

Asia Society and Museum
A Rockefeller sculpture collection combines with film, dance, and concerts.
725 Park Ave. at 70th St., tel 212/288-6400, $$$, asiasociety.org

Italian American Museum
This converted bank in Little Italy also served as a center for new arrivals.
155 Mulberry St., tel 212/ 965-9000, italianamerican museum.org

Tenement Museum
Take a guided tour (see pp. 30–31). **103 Orchard St., 877/975-3786, $$$$, tenement.org**

Downtown Shopping

Shopping in New York City is practically a contact sport, and nowhere is this more evident than in the boutiques and shopping throughways of downtown Manhattan. Stick to the main retail hubs below. Even if you're not buying, it's fun to see what trends are coming down the pipeline.

■ LOWER EAST SIDE

The Bowery marks the beginning of the Lower East Side, once home to a thriving Jewish community, today known for its nightlife and hip hotels. Boutiques around here trade in vintage cool. One such emporium is **Edith Machinist** *(104 Rivington St.)*, with its artfully curated clothes and accessories. Also visit **Assembly New York** *(170 Ludlow St.)*, which showcases rare designers alongside the Assembly brand upcycled and deadstock fabrics. Appease kids with a trip to **Economy Candy** *(108 Rivington St.)* for throwbacks like Jujubes and Whatchamacallit bars. End the expedition with a cocktail at the **Hotel on Rivington**'s first-floor bar *(107 Rivington St.)*.

■ SoHo

For both browsing and buying, SoHo is not to be missed. Peruse beautiful books at **McNally Jackson** *(52 Prince St.)*, and colorful multicultural housewares at **Global Table** *(107 Sullivan St.)*. Here, too, you'll find **Rag & Bone** *(119 Mercer St.)* for British-inspired clothing with a minimalist vibe. On Broadway, shopping gems include **Pearl River Mart** *(No. 452)*, an authentic Chinese department store that carries everything from traditional herbs to cheongsam dresses for toddlers.

■ NOLITA

Just east of Broadway lies Nolita (real-estate speak for "North of Little Italy"). Here, **Clare V.** *(239 Elizabeth St.)* is a must for women. The store sells chic clothing, bags, and accessories with a distinctly French flair. For outré fashion at similarly outré prices, visit **Ritual Vintage** *(377 Broome St.)*, which focuses on historical and vintage

Shoppers on trendy Bleecker Street in Greenwich Village in New York

designer women's clothing, shoes and accessories.

GREENWICH VILLAGE

Bleecker Street is ahead of the style curve with shops like **Intermix** *(No. 365)* for women's clothes and **Il Bisonte** *(No. 381)* for custom-made Italian leather goods. Since opening his boutique in 2001, Marc Jacobs has all but colonized the area—there's even a bookstore named **Bookmarc** *(No. 400)*. Prepare to be elbowed in the ribs by the perma-line of rabid shoppers at the tiny **Marc Jacobs Beauty** *(No. 385)*.

MEATPACKING DISTRICT

Amid the warehouses, lofts, and nightclubs just south of Chelsea, you'll find high-end designer boutiques on and around 14th Street, adding yet more glamour to this once-gritty locale. They include fashion heavyweight **Diane von Furstenberg** *(874 Washington St.)* and **Eberjey** *(13 Gansevoort St.)* for sophisticated lingerie, loungewear, resort and swimwear plus accessories. The fun continues with **Celine Jeffrey** *(449 West 49th St.)* fashionwear and insouciant French import, **Zadig & Voltaire** *(831 Washington St.)*.

The Villages

Famous for their colorful history, the East Village and Greenwich Village are linked but distinctive neighborhoods, bounded by 14th Street to the north and Houston Street to the south. The East Village, which stretches from Alphabet City in the east to Fourth Avenue and the Bowery in the west, was home to writers of the Beat Generation in the 1950s. With the rise of 1960s counterculture, hippies moved in where immigrants had once settled and created a new identity for this pocket of Lower Manhattan. Gentrification has brought in young professionals and families, but the East Village has kept its edginess and is still a great spot for an evening out. To the west, Greenwich Village combines a long tradition of bohemianism with some of the sharpest shopping and living spaces in its northwest corner, the Meatpacking District. At its heart, the area around Washington Square resounds with echoes of its literary past. Running from the Meatpacking District, the High Line—a park created from a former railroad—is a refreshing place to stroll and take in the views.

❍ **Street life in the East Village is relaxed and casual, in contrast to the elegance of uptown Manhattan.**

The Villages

These neighborhoods reveal New York's literary and offbeat sides, with lots of places to relax and admire the scene—and the people.

6 High Line

(see p. 63) New York's only elevated park has some of the best views of the city, especially at sunset.

5 Meatpacking District (see pp. 62–63) Trendy shops, clubs, and bars have transformed this area of former meat warehouses. Stop in at Chelsea Market, then make for the 14th Street entrance to the High Line.

THE VILLAGES   DISTANCE: APPROX. 5.5 MILES (9 KM)
TIME: APPROX. 7 HOURS   SUBWAY START: ASTOR PLACE

4 **Union Square Park** (see p. 62) New York's favorite farmers' market is held among statues of famous people in this park northeast of Greenwich Village. Head on toward the western end of West 14th Street.

3 **Greenwich Village** (see pp. 64–65) Ramble around this bohemian stronghold. From Washington Square, walk north on University Place.

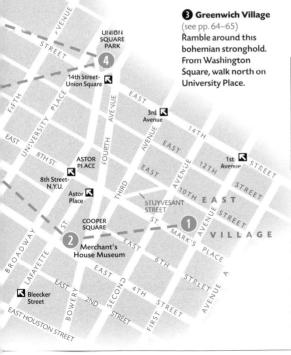

2 **Merchant's House Museum** (see p. 61) Lovingly curated rooms and funishings offer a glimpse into 19th-century city life in this time capsule on the borders of the East Village and Greenwich Village. Continue west on West Fourth Street.

1 **East Village** (see pp. 60–61) Start by exploring the streets of this lively, artsy area. From St. Mark's Place, walk south on Second Avenue then west on East Fourth Street.

THE VILLAGES

East Village

1 Once an immigrant neighborhood, the East Village acquired its distinctive feel in the 1960s as the haunt of artists, musicians, and hippies, and as the center of America's counterculture. Gentrification has erased some of the area's grittiness, but the neighborhood's artsy vibe is still evident in the graffiti-covered walls and independent stores. Street artist Jim Power has decorated almost all of the 80 lampposts with ceramics, mirrors, and glass: a new streetscape known as the **Mosaic Trail.**

At the heart of the village is **St. Mark's Place,** where vintage shops help keep the alternative spirit alive. One of the most famous, **Trash and Vaudeville** *(96 East 7th St.),* has been dressing rock stars and teenage rebels since 1975. St. Mark's Place ends at **Tompkins Square,** the scene of the first labor demonstration in 1874 and a performance space for Jimi Hendrix and other 1960s legends. Punk rock arrived in the 1970s, with bands such as the Ramones and

Strand Book Store, an independent bookstore at 828 Broadway, in the East Village.

Blondie regularly playing at the (now defunct) CBGB nightclub on the Bowery, once one of the slummiest areas of the city. The street's name derives from the *bouwerij* or farm belonging to the Dutch governor Peter Stuyvesant in the 17th century. He is buried at nearby **St. Mark's Church in-the-Bowery** (*131 East 10th St.*), one of New York's oldest churches. The East Village's Avenues A, B, C, and D—known as **Alphabet City**—have become a trendy enclave, with a nightlife that draws many uptowners.

Between East 14th and Houston Sts., and Broadway and Ave. D • Subway: 6 to Astor Pl.

Merchant's House Museum

2 A wealthy merchant family, the Tredwells, owned this Federal-style row house, built in 1832—the city's only 19th-century home to retain its original interior and exterior. Displayed in eight rooms over three floors are the family's fixtures and furnishings, decorative arts, and personal possessions. The museum is also reportedly Manhattan's most haunted house. Monthly, from January to October it presents Candlelight Ghost Tours; Gertrude Tredwell, the last owner, who died in 1933, is summoned from the great beyond.

29 East Fourth St., between the Bowery and Lafayette St. • tel 212/777-1089 • Closed Mon.-Wed., major holidays • $$$ • Subway: 6 to Astor Place • merchantshouse.org

Greenwich Village

3 See pp. 64–65.

Between Broadway and the Hudson River, and West 14th St. and Houston St. • Subway: A, B, C, D, E, F, V to West Fourth St.–Washington Square • nycgo.com

GOOD **EATS**

■ **CHELSEA MARKET**
This indoor market just north of Greenwich Village offers a huge range of gourmet food shopping, from delectable lobster to the perfect cup of coffee. **75 Ninth Ave., between West 15th and West 16th Sts., tel 212/652-2121**

■ **PRUNE**
Acclaimed chef Gabrielle Hamilton serves simple but sophisticated fare in this tiny, charming bistro. **54 East First St., between First and Second Aves., tel 212/677-6221, $$$$**

■ **UKRAINIAN EAST VILLAGE RESTAURANT**
Tap into the East Village's historic Ukrainian presence at this excellent folksy restaurant. **140 Second Ave., between East Ninth St. and St. Mark's Pl., tel 212/614-3283, $$**

THE VILLAGES

Union Square Park

4 Just north of Greenwich Village, Union Square lies at the intersection—or union—of Broadway and Fourth Avenue. Its 6.5-acre (2.6 ha) park has a popular **farmers' market,** where you can sample local bread, cheese, wine, and crafts on Mondays, Wednesdays, Fridays, and Saturdays. During November and December, the **Union Square Holiday Market** takes center stage, with stalls selling everything from jewelry and candles to ornaments and Christmas décor. Among the famous sculptures dotting the park is a bronze equestrian statue of first U.S. President George Washington. Cast in 1814, it is the oldest sculpture in New York City's park collection. Be sure to look up at the surrounding buildings to spot one of the city's most cherished landmarks: the kinetic **Metronome,** designed by artists Kristin Jones and Andrew Gizel. The piece features a digital clock and releases a continuous plume of steam.

14th St., at Broadway or Fourth Ave. • Subway: 4, 5, 6, L, N, Q, R to 14th St.–Union Sq. • nycgovparks.org

Meatpacking District

5 Once the home of the meat trade, this cluster of streets is now Manhattan's trendiest quarter and backdrop to some of the city's coolest restaurants, most exclusive clubs, and most expensive shops. You might even see a few meatpacking houses surviving among the modern glass architecture—snapshots of the area's past. Along 14th Street you can window-shop at the high-end boutiques of Diane von Furstenberg, Celine Jeffrey, and Christian Louboutin.

An exciting addiction to the neighborhood is the radically redesigned **Whitney Museum of American Art** *(99 Gansevoort St., tel 212/570-3600, $$$$$, whitney.org),* which boasts a prime spot between the Hudson and the High Line. Focusing on 20th-century and contemporary art, including works by Edward Hopper and Ray Lichtenstein, the museum has expansive gallery spaces and an education center outfitted with state-of-the-art classrooms and a 170-seat theater. Tasty treats of **Chelsea Market** *(chelseamarket.*

Touring the galleries of the Whitney Museum of American Art

com) lie just to the north of the district. Its 35-plus upscale food vendors include Saxelby for handcrafted American cheeses and Li-Lac for artisanal chocolates.

Between West 14th and Gansevoort Sts., and 10th Ave. and Hudson St.
• Subway: A, C, E, L to 14th St.–Eighth Ave. • meatpacking-district.com

High Line

6 This slimline park, 30 feet (9 m) above the ground, was created along 1.45 miles (2.3 km) of disused freight track. Miniature landscapes, such as wildflower meadows, adorn the walking trail from Gansevoort Street to West 34th Street; en route you can pause on wooden loungers and viewing platforms and admire temporary art installations. With views of the Hudson River and the streets below, the High Line is a special place to watch the sun set over the city.

Access at Gansevoort and Washington Sts., and every 2–3 blocks running north
• tel 212/500-6035 • Subway: A,C, E, L to 14th St.–Eighth Ave. • thehighline.org

Greenwich Village

The neighborhood's radical, bohemian spirit has attracted some of the most creative minds in politics and the arts since the early 19th century.

Washington Square Arch commemorates the centennial of the first president's inauguration.

New York's regular street pattern breaks up around Washington Square, home of New York University since 1835 and hub of Greenwich Village. Known to locals as "the Village," the world-famous neighborhood originally really was a village. By the late 19th century, literary salons, art clubs, and cutting-edge theaters were flourishing; by the end of World War I, residents and visitors included avant-garde figures such as Marcel Duchamp. As you walk the streets, catch up with the Village's vibrant music and intellectual scene, past and present.

WASHINGTON SQUARE PARK

At the head of the 10-acre (4 ha) park stands the **Washington Square Arch,** completed in 1895. In 1917, members of the left-leaning Liberal Club, including artist Marcel Duchamp, scaled the 86-foot-tall (26 m) arch and proclaimed the "Independent Republic of Greenwich Village."

MUSIC & COMEDY

Since 1962, New York's oldest rock club, **The Bitter End** *(147 Bleecker St. at LaGuardia Pl., tel 212/673-7030)* has been central to the area's music and comedy scenes. Bob Dylan, Stevie Wonder, and Woody Allen, among others, all performed here. **Café Wha?** *(115 Macdougal St., between Bleecker and West 3rd Sts., tel 212/254-3706)* also attracted major musical and comedy talents, from Bruce Springsteen to Richard Pryor. Its house bands and guest musicians still pump out styles from jazz, soul, and R&B to modern and alternative. Don't miss a visit to the **Duplex** *(61 Christopher St.; tel 212/255-5438),* a neighborhood standby with multiple stages featuring a piano bar, cabaret, and more. **The Stonewall Inn** *(53 Christopher St. at Seventh Ave.,*

tel 212/488-2705) proclaims itself the birthplace of the gay liberation movement, after a police raid triggered the Stonewall riots of June 1969. Gay cabaret, karaoke, and comedy shows are all part of the lineup in the renovated bar.

WRITERS' VILLAGE

Close to Washington Square, charming **Patchin Place** was home to poet e. e. cummings, playwright Eugene O'Neill, and journalist John Reed. Drop in at cozy **Caffe Reggio** *(119 Macdougal St., tel 212/475-9557)* to sip a cappuccino where Jack Kerouac hung out. Theater lovers can sample New York's oldest Off-Broadway venue, **Cherry Lane Theatre** *(38 Commerce St., tel 212/989-2020),* where plays by F. Scott Fitzgerald, Tennessee Williams, and Samuel Beckett debuted.

THE VILLAGES

Between Broadway and the Hudson River, and West 14th St. and Houston St. • Subway: A, B, C, D, E, F, V to West Fourth St.–Washington Square • nycgo.com

City of Writers

From its early days, Greenwich Village has attracted some of the greatest names in American literature, including Mark Twain and Edgar Allan Poe. This phenomenon continued throughout the 20th century, while authors from around the world also swelled the throng. But ever since a native literature began to flourish on the continent, virtually every neighborhood in the city can claim to have housed a celebrated poet, novelist, playwright, or journalist.

Allen Ginsberg was snapped by his friend William Burroughs on their East Village apartment rooftop in 1953 (above). Before being colonized by writers, the White Horse Tavern (right) was a longshoremen's bar.

Beginnings

New York's literary roots can be traced to Washington Irving, considered the first American to make a living from writing. Famous for the short story "Rip Van Winkle," Irving was born and raised in post-colonial Manhattan. In 1807 Irving launched the satirical literary magazine *Salmagundi,* in which he coined the term "Gotham" as a pseudonym for New York.

Walt Whitman moved to Brooklyn with his family in 1824 and, by age 11, was working in the local newspaper business. After various travels outside of New York, he returned to Brooklyn and published his collection of free-flowing poems, *Leaves of Grass,* in 1855. His contemporary, Herman Melville, author of *Moby-Dick,* worked for many years as a New York City customs inspector.

Mark Twain was senior partner in the publishing company Charles L. Webster & Co., based in Union Square, until bad investments obliged him to file for bankruptcy. Having recouped his fortunes, he returned to New York in 1900.

Modern Greats

After World War I, wit and writer Dorothy Parker was the best-known member of the Algonquin Round Table, which met at the Algonquin Hotel (see p. 183). Her friend, Brooklyn-born humorist S. J. Perelman, was a regular contributor to *The New Yorker* magazine, founded in 1925. That year also saw the publication of *Manhattan Transfer,* John Dos Passos's novel inspired by New York life.

By the 1950s, New York was abuzz with literary talent, including poet Allen Ginsberg and novelists Jack Kerouac and Norman Mailer. Truman Capote published *Breakfast at Tiffany's* in 1958. James Baldwin published *Another Country,* set in Harlem and Greenwich Village, in 1962. In recent decades, figures such as the Bronx-born Don DeLillo and Brooklyn resident Paul Auster have dominated the city's literary scene.

LITERARY
WATERING HOLES

Kettle of Fish
Ginsberg, Kerouac, and friends spent many a happy night in this still popular neighborhood bar in Greenwich Village. **59 Christopher St., tel 212/414-2278**

Minetta Tavern
Opened in Greenwich Village in 1937, this now renovated restaurant once drew poet Ezra Pound and novelist Ernest Hemingway. **113 Macdougal St., tel 212/475-3850**

White Horse Tavern
In western Greenwich Village, the White Horse was a favorite with novelists Norman Mailer, James Baldwin, and Anaïs Nin. **567 Hudson St. at 11th St., tel 212/989-3956**

Jazz Clubs

New York has been a magnet for jazz acts and aficionados since the early 20th century. From big bands in 1940s Harlem, to the bebop of the 1950s and 1960s, to innovators of avant-garde in the Village, the history of this lively music traverses the city from one end to the other.

■ GREENWICH VILLAGE & THE LOWER EAST SIDE

Arguably the most famous jazz club in the world, the **Blue Note** (*131 West Third St. between Sixth Ave. and Macdougal St., tel 212/475-8592*) was founded in 1981 and is the number-one choice for seeing big-name acts in an intimate setting. Just around the corner is the **Village Vanguard** (*178 Seventh Ave S. at Perry St., tel 212/255-4037*), unmissable if only because it is where saxophonist John Coltrane made his famous 1961 live recordings. **Smalls** (*183 West 10th St. at West Fourth St., tel 646/476-4346*) promises an authentic club experience—a hole-in-the-wall basement space that presents up-and-coming talent. Over in the East Village, **The Stone** (*55 West 13th St., closed Sun.-Tue., thestonenyc.com*) is a not-for-profit space dedicated to avant-garde and experimental jazz.

■ MIDTOWN

One of the hottest Midtown clubs, **The Iridium** (*1650 Broadway at 51st St., tel 212/582-2121*) became famous for its weekly sessions with the late jazz guitarist Les Paul. The Les Paul Trio still play here on occasions, often alongside such greats as José Feliciano. Named for saxophonist Charlie "Bird" Parker, **Birdland** (*315 West 44th St., between Ninth and Eighth Aves., tel 212/581-3080*) carries on a 70-year tradition of bringing together big bands. For jazz with stunning scenery, head to **Dizzy's Club** (*10 Columbus Circle, tel 212/258-9595*) on the fifth floor of the Lincoln Center. It commands both a staggering view of Central Park and great jazz acts.

■ UPPER WEST SIDE

Newly transformed and expanded during the COVID pandemic, **Smoke Jazz Club** (*2751 Broadway,*

Guitarists Jeff Beck and Brian Setzer play at The Iridium as part of a tribute to Les Paul.

tel. 212/864-6662, smokejazz.com)
reopened in 2022 with the George
Coleman Quartet and special guest
Peter Bernstein, plus such megastars as
the Eddie Henderson Quintet, Mary
Stallings in its lineup.

■ HARLEM
The historic heart of New York's jazz
scene still boasts some of the city's
best venues. **Minton's** (206 W. 118th
St., tel 212/866-1262), a storied
venue considered to be the birthplace
of bebop, has featured all the jazz
heavyweights, from Charlie Parker to
Thelonius Monk. For a more intimate
experience, try catching a jam session
at **American Legion Post 398** (248
West 132nd St., between Seventh and
Eighth Aves., tel 212/283-9701). In
a tiny basement of a brownstone, this
friendly venue serves up excellent soul
food, as well as accomplished jazz. (For
more Harlem clubs, see p. 157.)

■ BROOKLYN
From Manhattan, a short hop on
the F train to Park Slope in west
Brooklyn takes you to French-owned
Barbès (376 Ninth St. at Sixth Ave.,
tel 347/422-0248), where local and
international jazz is often happening.

Midtown South

Midtown South runs between the two rivers and between 42nd and 14th Streets. During the boom years of the 19th century, this area was the city's commercial epicenter, and here the soaring Empire State Building and other art deco masterpieces rose into the air, forging both the modern skyscraper and the Manhattan skyline. There is much to delight the visitor at street level, too—the historic Gramercy Park neighborhood is great for a quiet stroll past stately brownstones and converted carriage houses. Fifth Avenue fashion emporiums rival the attractions of museums displaying rare artifacts. New York Public Library's marble lions protect a Gutenberg Bible and the real Winnie the Pooh; the Morgan Library & Museum houses the manuscript and art collection of 19th-century banker Pierpont Morgan; and the Rubin Museum of Art displays masterpieces from the Far East. For lunch, savor the city's finest spicy food in the Indian restaurants that line Curry Hill, the section of Lexington Avenue between 20th and 29th Streets.

◗ **Madison Square Park provides one of Midtown South's peaceful places to slow down and admire the towering Empire State Building.**

Midtown South

New York's tallest skyscraper looms over this district of quiet parks, busy shops, and museums filled with priceless artifacts.

❶ Rubin Museum of Art (see p. 74) This museum of art from Himalayan countries houses a mask of the Hindu god Shiva in his fierce form. Make your way up Seventh Avenue, then west on West 23rd Street.

❷ Hotel Chelsea (see pp. 74–75) Writers and rock stars have called this bohemian hotel home. Head down West 23rd Street to Fifth Avenue.

❸ Flatiron Building (see pp. 75–76) The 285-foot-high (87 m) forerunner of the skyscraper tapers to less than 6 feet (2 m) wide at the front. Walk south on Broadway and turn right on East 20th Street.

WEST
WEST
WEST 40TH
WEST AVENUE 38TH
WEST AVENUE 36TH
WEST AVENUE
WEST 34TH

34th Street-
Penn Station

WEST 30TH STREET

CHELSEA PARK
WEST 28TH STREET
WEST 26TH STREET
28th Street
CHELSEA
WEST 23RD
23rd Street
Hotel Chelsea ❷ ST.
23rd Street 23rd Street
WEST 20TH STREET
WEST OF
18th Street
17TH WEST
14th Street
Rubin Museum of Art ❶
8th Avenue 14TH 14th Street AVENUE STREET
6th Avenue 14th Street STREET

TENTH AVENUE
NINTH AVENUE
EIGHTH STREET
SEVENTH

0   600 meters
0   600 yards

MIDTOWN SOUTH   DISTANCE: 2.9 MILES (4.6 KM)
TIME: APPROX. 6.5 HOURS   SUBWAY START: 18TH ST.–7TH AVE.

❽ New York Public Library (see pp. 80–81) The imposing marble building is home to one of the world's most extensive book collections.

GARMENT DISTRICT

42nd Street

42nd Street-Times Square

42nd Street

BRYANT PARK

5th Avenue

New York Public Library ❽

Grand Central-42nd Street

34th Street-Penn Station

HERALD SQUARE

34th Street

Empire State Building

GREELEY SQUARE

Morgan Library & Museum ❼

❻

MURRAY HILL

33rd Street

28th Street

28th Street

MADISON SQUARE PARK

❺

23rd Street

23rd Street

Flatiron Building

❸

❹

Gramercy Park

UNION SQUARE

14th Street-Union Square

STUYVESANT SQUARE

3rd Avenue

1st Avenue

❼ Morgan Library & Museum (see pp. 78–79) Banker Pierpont Morgan's collection of cultural treasures includes rare manuscripts, books, prints, drawings, and paintings. Continue up Fifth Avenue to 42nd Street.

❻ Empire State Building (see p. 78) Manhattan's most famous, this skyscraper affords sweeping views of the city. Farther up Fifth Avenue, turn right on East 36th Street.

❺ Madison Square Park (see p. 77) Spend some carefree time in this urban oasis of greenery. Follow Fifth Avenue north to East 34th Street.

❹ Gramercy Park (see pp. 76–77) This neighborhood features quaint town houses and architectural gems along tree-lined streets. From Park Avenue South, turn left on East 23rd Street.

Rubin Museum of Art

1 The Western world's first and largest museum dedicated to Himalayan culture holds more than 2,000 items. They include pieces dating from the second to the 20th centuries from the mountainous regions between Afghanistan and Myanmar (Burma). A steel-and-marble spiral staircase winds up through the seven-story building to galleries that display Buddhist sculptures, vibrant Tibetan *thangkas* (scroll paintings), ornate geometric paintings called mandalas, carved masks, and skillfully woven textiles. On the third floor, the regularly rotating exhibit "Masterworks: Jewels of the Collection" showcases outstanding works of art, such as a **14th-century Nepali Buddha;** a Tibetan bronze of a divine couple, **"Samvara in Union with Vajrayogini";** and photographic reproductions of the rarely seen **Lukhang Murals** in the temple of the Dalai Lamas in Lhasa, Tibet. On Friday evenings, the Rubin's Café Serai becomes the **K2 Lounge,** and you can choose savory cuisine from a menu of Pan-Asian snacks while listening to a live DJ.

150 West 17th St., between Sixth and Seventh Aves. • tel 212/620-5000 • Closed Mon.-Wed., Jan. 1, Thanksgiving, Dec. 25 • $$ • Subway: 1 to 18th St.–7th Ave. • rubinmuseum.org

Hotel Chelsea

2 During the 1950s and '60s, artists, musicians, and writers hung out at the Chelsea Hotel (popularly known as Hotel Chelsea) in what had become a bohemian commune. Originally built in 1883 as a private apartment cooperative, the 12-story, Victorian redbrick Gothic building with florid cast-iron balconies became a hotel in 1905. The famed venue has played host to such musical luminaries as Bob Dylan, Patti Smith, Jimi Hendrix, and Janis Joplin, as well as many writers—Arthur Miller and Gore Vidal among them. Songs, stories, and novels have been written both in and about the hotel, including *2001: A Space Odyssey,* which Arthur C. Clarke penned while staying here. It was also

Fifth Avenue Clock and Flatiron Building in the background

here that years of heavy drinking caught up with the Welsh poet, Dylan Thomas, who died after collapsing at the hotel following a visit to the White Horse Tavern in Greenwich Village. Perhaps the most infamous event to happen there was the murder of Nancy Spungen, possibly by her boyfriend—Sex Pistols bass player Sid Vicious. History aside, the hotel reopened in 2021 after a massive decade-long (and strife-filled) renovation that saw the developers battling the city and tenants.

222 West 23rd St., between Seventh and Eighth Aves. • tel 212/483-1010 • $$$
• Subway: 1 to 23rd St.–7th Ave. or C, E to 23rd St.–8th Ave. • hotelchelsea.com

Flatiron Building

3 The triangular sliver of land formed by the intersection of Fifth Avenue, Broadway, and 23rd Street dictated the foundation for this oddly shaped structure, completed in 1902. Designed by Daniel H. Burnham & Co. (of Chicago World's Fair fame) and originally named the Fuller Building, this early skyscraper has a three-sided configuration that led to its current name—the Flatiron Building. A National Historic Landmark, it was one of the first structures constructed with a steel frame that formed a strong foundation for its exterior walls—an architectural principle employed in many later skyscrapers. Ornate geometric decorations are interspersed with terra-cotta faces that peer down at passersby. The Flatiron has been vacant since a renovation of its innards began in 2019, but the ground floor stores remain open.

175 Fifth Ave., between 22nd and 23rd Sts. • Subway: N, R to 23rd St.

Gramercy Park

4 This tree-lined neighborhood of architectural beauty was a swamp before it was laid out as one of New York's most attractive residential areas in 1822. The stretch of 19th Street between Irving Place and Third Avenue, with its many mid-19th-century town houses, was dubbed the "Block Beautiful." It was once home to artists and writers including journalist Ida Tarbell. Elegant mansions grace the square: **The Players** club (*16 Gramercy Park*)—once residence of Shakespearean actor Edwin Booth (brother of Abraham Lincoln's assassin John Wilkes Booth)— was renovated by architect Stanford White. At 15 Gramercy Park, the **National Arts Club** is housed in a mansion once owned by New York governor Samuel Tilden. Prestigious club members have included writer Mark Twain, poet W.H. Auden, and sculptor Augustus Saint-Gaudens. The park that gives its name to the area remains closed to all but residents and Gramercy Park Hotel guests. Peek through the gates for a glimpse of its lush greenery. Saunter south one block for drinks at

Edwin Booth's popularity as the leading actor of his day survived his brother's notoriety, and he is honored in Gramercy Park.

Pete's Tavern (*129 East 18th St. at Irving Pl.*), one of New York's oldest bars, where writer O. Henry wrote his short story "The Gift of the Magi" in 1904. To the west is the **Theodore Roosevelt Birthplace**—a reconstruction of the house on this site where the U.S. president was born.

From 17th to 22nd Sts., between Park Ave. South and Third Ave. • Subway: 4, 6 to 23rd St. or 4, 5, 6, L, N, Q, R to Union Sq.

Madison Square Park

5 The vibrant, verdant ground that stretches from 23rd to 26th Streets between Madison and Fifth Avenues has been a dedicated public space since 1686. The six-acre (2.4 ha) park has a significant role in baseball's history; the city's first team, the New York Knickerbockers, formed here in 1845, before it opened as Madison Square Park two years later. Today, benches are set among shady trees, historic statuary, and year-round public art. **Bridget's Garden,** on the park's northern side, has a playground, while **Lilac Grove** brims with rare yellow primrose lilacs.

If you're hungry, join the lines at **Shake Shack** (*near Madison Ave. and East 23rd St., shakeshack. com, $*), on the southern end of the park, which serves burgers, a vegetarian Portobello creation, frozen custard, and, of course, shakes, floats, and frozen custard. In summertime, free concerts send jazz, folk, and other music drifting through the air, and informal art talks are hosted. Free family-friendly wildlife walks and "Fireflies at Dusk" watch parties are also offered.

East 23rd to East 26th Sts., between Fifth and Madison Aves. • tel 212/520-7600; Subway: 6, F, N, R to 23rd St. • madisonsquarepark.org

GOOD **EATS**

■ **BHATTI INDIAN GRILL**
Enjoy authentic North Indian cuisine, from spicy curries to savory kebabs, at this elegant upscale restaurant.
100 Lexington Ave. at 27th St., tel 212/683-4228, $$$

■ **DHABA**
Savor Southern Indian food with dishes for vegetarians and meat-eaters alike.
108 Lexington Ave. between 27th and 28th Sts., tel 212/679-1284, $$$

■ **PENELOPE**
A cozy café serving soups, salads, and sandwiches.
159 Lexington Ave. at 30th St., tel 212/481-3800, $$$

■ **PONGAL**
This small restaurant serves Indian cuisine at good prices.
110 Lexington Ave., tel 212/696-9458, $$$

MIDTOWN SOUTH

Empire State Building

6 Soaring 1,454 feet (443 m) into the New York City skyline, this art deco masterpiece, completed in 1931, reigned supreme for more than four decades as the world's tallest building. From scenes of King Kong scaling the structure to the poignant stories of *An Affair to Remember* and *Sleepless in Seattle*, it has provided a favorite backdrop for movie directors. Upon entering, stroll through the **ornate lobby,** where restored gold-leaf-on-canvas murals of the sun and planets grace the expansive ceiling. The walls feature painted panels of the Seven Wonders of the Ancient World. Amble over to the street level **State Grill and Bar,** which serves breakfast, lunch, and dinner with an emphasis on New York State ingredients. You can unwind here before taking the high-speed elevators to the **86th floor observatory,** or, for an extra fee, the **102nd floor observatory.** The last elevator leaves at 1:15 a.m., allowing for spectacular nighttime vistas of the millions of twinkling city lights. To dig deeper into the history behind the building, check out such permanent exhibitions as **Construction,** which places you amid the noisy action of 1902s work crews as they move steel beams into place.

350 Fifth Ave., between 33rd and 34th Sts. • tel 212/736-3100 • Observatory tickets: $$$$$ • Subway: D, F, N,Q, R to 34th St.–Herald Square • esbnyc.com

Morgan Library & Museum

7 Financier Pierpont Morgan amassed an extraordinary collection of rare artwork, literature, and music memorabilia. Among its treasures are illuminated medieval and Renaissance manuscripts, a signed manuscript of a Mozart symphony, and the only serving manuscript of Milton's *Paradise Lost*. Such items are displayed on a rotating basis. Charles Dickens's manuscript of *A Christmas Carol* is always on view around Christmas, while permanent displays include **Ancient Mesopotamian tablets and seals** from 3000 B.C. onward. The fine art includes works on paper by Rembrandt and Peter Paul Rubens. In 1924, after the financier's death, his son J. P. Morgan, Jr.,

The Morgan Library's rotunda has a marble floor and columns of Renaissance inspiration.

gave the library to the public. Housed in a 1906 Renaissance-style villa designed by Charles McKim, it has a **rotunda** with an ornately decorated ceiling and inlaid marble floor. The Morgan campus also includes a light-filled courtyard by noted Italian architect Renzo Piano that connects the library's three main buildings. Pause here to unwind, or attend a concert, lecture, or other live performance in the lower-level **Gilder Lehrman Hall,** and special events for children include a Winter Family Fair. Casual dining awaits in the **Morgan Café.**

225 Madison Ave. at 36th St. • tel 212/685-0008 • Closed Mon., Jan. 1, Thanksgiving, and Dec. 25 • $$$$$ • Subway: 6 to 33rd St. • themorgan.org

New York Public Library

8 See pp. 80–81.

Fifth Ave. at 42nd St. • tel 917/275-6975 • Closed all public holidays • Subway: 7 to Fifth Ave. or 1, 2, 3, 7, N, Q, R, S to Times Sq.–42nd St., or D, F to 42nd St. Bryant Park • nypl.org

New York Public Library

*See one of America's foremost libraries—with a Bible that changed the
world and a bear who enriched countless children's childhoods.*

The handsome Lionel Pincus and Princess Firyal Map Division

A massive temple to all things literary, the Stephen A. Schwarzman Building—
better known as the main branch of the New York Public Library—opened in
1911. As well as housing 8.7 million treasured artifacts and books, the library
has one of the world's longest and most famous reading rooms, loved by
writers such as Norman Mailer and Alfred Kazin. The beaux arts building,
designed by architects Carrère and Hastings, was designated a National
Historic Landmark in 1965.

■ THE LIBRARY LIONS

Standing guard at the library's entrance are Patience and Fortitude—marble lions designed by sculptor Edward Clark Potter and carved by a family of well-known marble cutters, the Piccirilli brothers. Mayor Fiorello LaGuardia gave the lions their names in the 1930s, after the qualities he felt New Yorkers needed during the Great Depression.

■ THE REAL WINNIE THE POOH

Although Christopher Robin named his cuddly toy Edward, it was as Winnie the Pooh that he became the world's most popular bear. The original stuffed animal, a first-birthday present from his father, A.A. Milne, resides in the **Children's Center,** with his friends Piglet, Eeyore, Tigger, and Kanga.

■ GUTENBERG BIBLE

Taking pride of place in the library's **Rare Book Division** is a Gutenberg Bible, printed around 1455. German publisher Johannes Gutenberg invented the printing press around 1440. Some 180 Gutenberg Bibles were originally produced, yet only 48 survive. The story goes that when this rare tome arrived from Europe, New

SAVVY **TRAVELER**

Don't miss the free, one-hour guided tours at 11 a.m. and 2 p.m., Monday through Saturday, and 1:30 p.m. and 3 p.m. on Sundays. Meet at the reception desk.

York Customs House officials were required to remove their hats in honor of the holy book.

■ MAPPING THE WORLD

The **Lionel Pincus and Princess Firyal Map Division** in the northeast corner of the building has lofty ceilings with ornate golden molding, elegant chandeliers, and massive arched windows. Established in 1898, the collection includes more than 400,000 maps and 20,000 books and atlases dating from the 15th to 21st centuries.

■ BRYANT PARK

Behind the building lies a verdant expanse used for the 1853 Crystal Palace Fair. The park provides multicolored blossoms, a twirling carousel, and numerous eateries. In summer enjoy a free concert, and in winter go ice skating or visit the holiday market (see p. 101).

MIDTOWN SOUTH

Fifth Ave. at 42nd St. • tel 917/275-6975 • Closed all public holidays • Subway: 7 to Fifth Ave. or 1, 2, 3, 7, N, Q, R, S to Times Sq.–42nd St., or D, F to 42nd St. Bryant Park • nypl.org

A Passion for Fashion

With many of the world's top designers making New York their home, the Big Apple offers fashion retail therapy like nowhere else. If you're passionate about what you wear, explore the haute-couture fashion houses along with numerous independent shops. You'll find famous names such as Calvin Klein, Vera Wang, and Marc Jacobs, while many of the smaller boutiques promise cutting-edge designs and new talent.

Happy shoppers pause for a breath on legendary Madison Avenue (above). Detail of Diane von Furstenberg store. Gucci's store (opposite) adds a shimmer to Fifth Avenue.

Growing Fame

The Fashion (or Garment) District is a small neighborhood, running from 34th Street and Fifth Avenue to 42nd Street and Ninth Avenue. The area was originally known for manufacturing uniforms for sailors, farm workers, and Union soldiers during the Civil War. With industrialization and an improved economy came the demand for an industry to outfit American families.

By the early 20th century, factories here were making the majority of women's clothing in the United States. New York's first Fashion Week, which was held during World War II, drew attention to the new industry. Now the shows that make up Fashion Week are held twice a year, helping promote American designs to the world.

Stylish Education

The rise in the fashion economy led to the founding of the Fashion Institute of Technology (FIT) in 1944. Today, FIT is considered one of the world's top fashion schools, with alumni including

Calvin Klein, Ralph Rucci, and Reem Acra. The institute's museum displays garments from the 18th century to the present day *(Seventh Ave. at 27th St., tel 212/217-4558, closed Sun. and Mon., fitnyc.edu).*

Fashion Shopping

Pay homage to Cartier, Gucci, Harry Winston, Louis Vuitton, Saks Fifth Avenue, Tiffany & Co., and many more iconic shops along **Fifth Avenue.** A trip downtown (see pp. 54–55) brings you to **SoHo,** where mainstream brands mix with vendors on Broadway selling handcrafted pieces. The retail scene includes trendy French fashion stores, such as **A.P.C.** *(131 Mercer St.)* for culty jeans and apparel, and cult-label **Céline** *(67 Wooster St.)* for trendy minimalist bags and apparel.

DESIGNER **STUDIOS**

Go straight to the source for skillfully crafted designer items.

Alexander McQueen
Shop here for skull-embellished scarves, edgy garments, boss shoes, and runway collections.
747 Madison Ave., tel 212/645-1797

Diane von Furstenberg
A one-stop shop for wrap dresses, shoes, and accessories.
874 Washington St. at W. 14th St., tel 646/486-4800

Michael Andrews Bespoke
Visit this cozy shop for custom-designed menswear.
2 Great Jones Alley, between Lafayette and Broadway., tel 212/677-1755

MIDTOWN SOUTH

Bars & Cocktails

America's biggest city does socializing very well. Locals enjoy a brunch, power lunch, or post-work or pre-dinner cocktail, especially when it's artfully crafted. Whether you prefer a centuries-old tavern, a hidden underground den, or a rooftop lounge, there is always the perfect place to quench your thirst.

■ CHIC & SLEEK

In Midtown East, the art deco-esque **Ophelia Lounge** (*3 Mitchell Place, tel 212/980-4796*) atop the Beekman Tower offers wraparound city views, and such Instagram-worthy cocktails as Ophelia's Ascension, with pepper-infused mezcal and bourbon.

Upstairs at The Kimberly (*145 East 50th St., between Third and Lexington Aves., tel 212/888-1220*) is one of Midtown North's hidden gems. Relax in this rooftop lounge, presided over by mixologist Alex Ott, and enjoy a 360-degree vista of the city.

■ OLD SCHOOL

The oldest continuously operating bar in the city, **McSorley's Old Ale House** (*15 E. 7th St., tel 212/473-9148*), opened in 1854, is a no-frills, covered-in-dust saloon with just two house-made brews on offer: light and dark. Order the hamburger or chili and leave your credit cards behind—it's cash only.

■ INSPIRED SPEAKEASIES

Although forbidden cocktail dens are a distant memory of the Prohibition Era, speakeasys are not. Enter Greenwich Village's **Little Branch** (*20 Seventh Ave. South at St. Lukes Pl., tel 212/929-4360*), founded by famed mixologist Sasha Petraske (1973-2015). Downstairs, you'll find a dimly lit bar with knowledgeable tenders.

Once inside **Crif Dogs,** a hotdog shop in the East Village, you might think you've landed in the wrong place. Look a little closer, and you'll notice a telephone booth leading to **P.D.T.,** which stands for "Please Don't Tell" (*113 St. Marks Pl., between First Ave. and Ave. A, tel 212/614-0386*). In this tiny underground bar with a devoted following, you'll find an innovative menu featuring creative pairings such as bacon-infused whiskey with maple syrup and a twist of orange.

MIDTOWN SOUTH

Cocktails are expertly mixed at the minuscule, subterranean P.D.T. in the East Village.

■ WINE & BEER

Long, banquet-style tasting tables set the tone in East Village's **Terroir Tribeca** (*24 Harrison St. at Greenwich St., tel 212/625-9463*). You'll receive your menu in a notebook filled with wine lists and amusing articles and political commentaries. A small-plates menu, heavy on cheese and charcuterie, complements the wines.

The cobblestone Meatpacking District gets a bit of whimsical fun at the **Biergarten** of **The Standard** hotel (*848 Washington St. at West 13th St., tel 212/645-4646*). Hotelier André Balazs combines ping-pong tables, sophisticated clientele, and plastic furniture with stunning views of the High Line—an elevated former railroad that has been transformed into a park (see p. 63).

Chef Daniel Boulud brings world-class wines to the Upper West Side at **Bar Boulud** (*1900 Broadway, at 64th St., tel 212/595-0303*). You can sample from a carefully curated list of more than 50 wines, many from the Rhône Valley and Burgundy. Housemade charcuterie and Lyonnais-style dishes help the wines shine even more.

Midtown North

Midtown North touches both the Hudson and East Rivers, and is bounded by Central Park on the north and 42nd Street on the south. The sidewalks of this vibrant area bustle with office workers, shoppers cruising Fifth Avenue boutiques, and both locals and tourists flocking to Times Square's theaters and restaurants. Wall Street might carry New York's financial muscle, but the bulk of the city's corporate and cultural power is anchored in Midtown North, hub of publishing and broadcasting.

Much of what the nation reads and watches emanates from its steel-and-glass heights and neon-studded canyons. And worldwide, billions of people are affected by decisions made at the United Nations headquarters on the East River waterfront. The architecture demands your upward gaze at such world-renowned landmarks as the art deco Chrysler Building and Rockefeller Center. Representing the fine arts is the Museum of Modern Art, its recently expanded and renovated space a perfect showcase for its dazzling collection.

◑ The neo-Gothic twin spires of St. Patrick's Cathedral loom 330 feet (100.5 m) above Fifth Avenue, a captivating contrast to sleek skyscrapers.

Midtown North

Walk from river to river to view magnificent skyscrapers, the city's glitzy theater district, and its unparalleled modern art collection.

MIDTOWN NORTH

① Intrepid Sea, Air & Space Museum (see p. 90) Veteran of three wars and the space race, the aircraft carrier *Intrepid* is the museum's centerpiece. Also on exhibit are a nuclear submarine and supersonic Concorde plane. Make your way five blocks east on 46th Street.

② Times Square (see pp. 90–91) Hub of New York's theater district, this major crossroads provides endless entertainment. From the south end of the square, walk east along 42nd Street.

③ Madame Tussauds (see p. 92) Meet more than 200 lifelike figures of wax from the world of politics, sports, and the arts, including Lady Gaga. Backtrack through Times Square and go east on 49th Street.

MIDTOWN NORTH   DISTANCE: APPROX. 3 MILES (4.8 KM)
TIME: APPROX. 8 HOURS   SUBWAY: 42ND ST.

❹ Rockefeller Center
(see pp. 92–93) **This city within a city** includes the Top of the Rock observation deck, Radio City Music Hall, and, in winter, the celebrated ice rink in Rockefeller Plaza. Head north along Avenue of the Americas and then east along 53rd Street.

❺ Museum of Modern Art
(see pp. 96–97) **The world's richest modern art trove,** MoMA's collection spans Postimpressionism to cutting-edge digital expression. Walk half a block east along 53rd Street and then one block south on Fifth Avenue.

❻ St. Patrick's Cathedral
(see pp. 93–94) **Manhattan's masterful Catholic cathedral** provides a quiet respite from the Midtown mayhem. Continue south along Fifth Avenue and east along 42nd Street.

❼ Grand Central Terminal
(see p. 94) **New York's temple of transportation** bustles night and day with commuters and people who come to admire its vast expanses and beaux arts details. Continue east along 42nd Street.

❽ Chrysler Building (see p. 94) **Art deco meets the Age of the Automobile** in the skyscraper with the silver spire, tallest building in the world until the Empire State Building was completed in 1931. Continue east along 42nd Street.

❾ United Nations Headquarters
(see p. 95) **A monument to both modern architecture** and aspirations to world harmony, the UN complex has been part of the East River skyline since 1952.

MIDTOWN NORTH

Intrepid Sea, Air & Space Museum

1 After serving in World War II, Korea, and Vietnam, the U.S.S. *Intrepid* (CVS-11) found a permanent home alongside Pier 86 on the Hudson River. Here it metamorphosed from a fighting machine into a wide-ranging museum devoted to mankind's achievements on the water, in the air, and even in outer space. Get up close and personal with nearly two dozen **military aircraft** on the carrier's flight deck and a supersonic **Concorde.** Test your aviation skills in an A-6 fighter-jet flight simulator, and relive the infamous day in 1944 when the carrier survived direct hits by two Japanese kamikaze planes. The space exhibits may seem out of place here, but they are actually very relevant to the vessel's history, since U.S.S. *Intrepid* served as the recovery ship on several Mercury and Gemini space missions. Visitors can tour the carrier on their own or join guided tours to see behind-the-scenes stops that are not accessible otherwise. Tied up beside the flattop (and also open to visitors) is the ***Growler,*** the world's oldest surviving nuclear missile submarine.

Pier 86, West 46th St. and 12th Ave. • tel 212/245-0072 • Closed Thanksgiving, Dec. 25 • $$$$$ (includes admission to *Growler*), extra charges for simulator rides • Subway: A, C, E to 42nd St.–Port Authority Bus Terminal • intrepidmuseum.org

Times Square

2 Gazing up at the neon-lit billboards and theater marquees as a current of pedestrians and traffic swirls by, you have the overwhelming sense that Times Square really is the "Crossroads of the World." More than a million people gather each New Year's Eve to watch the Waterford crystal ball on the One Times Square skyscraper mark the start of a new year.

It's hard to imagine nowadays, but the square was once the outer edge of civilization, a collection of liveries and stables where many New Yorkers kept their horses and buggies. By the end of the 19th century, the first theaters had begun to appear, and by the early 20th century, this section of Broadway had been dubbed the Great White

Zoning ordinances require Times Square businesses to display illuminated signs.

Way (after its brilliant lighting). But over time patrons fled the area for other Manhattan temptations, and by the late 1960s, Times Square had become a realm of dive bars, sex shops, and X-rated venues. In the 1990s a concerted effort by both public and private sectors sought to revive the area.

Times Square glimmers once again as a place to shop, play, eat, or just watch the world walk by. Family-friendly attractions include the giant **Disney Store** (*1540 Broadway*) keeps the magic going with its costumed cartoon and MARVEL characters and three floors of Disney toys and apparel. **MTV**'s glass-fronted bastion (*1515 Broadway between 44th and 45th Sts.*) attracts hordes of eager teens daily. Tourists flock to the **TKTS discount ticket booth** in refurbished Duffy Square and elbow their way into local restaurants for quick pre-theater eats.

Intersection of Broadway and Seventh Ave. • Subway: 1, 2, 3, 7, N, Q, R, S to 42nd St.–Times Sq. • timessquarenyc.org

Madame Tussauds

3 This New York version of the venerable London waxworks does its best to keep pace with ever-changing pop culture. More than 200 wax creations are complemented by a Film & TV space that invites you into scenes from classic movies, like *E.T.*, a Sports Zone with interactive games, and a Marvel Super Heroes 4D Film Experience, featuring comic faves like the Hulk and Ironman.

234 West 42nd St., between Seventh and Eighth Aves. • tel 212/512-9600 • $$$$$ • Subway: 1, 2, 3, N, Q, R to 42nd St.–Times Sq. • madametussauds.com/new-york

Rockefeller Center

4 Oil fortune heir John D. Rockefeller, Jr., hatched the idea of a grand cultural, commercial, and entertainment complex on a large Midtown property he was leasing from Columbia University. The task of creating this "city within a city" was handed to Wallace K.

Harrison, whose team helped construct 19 buildings, ranging from immensely tall to surprisingly short, fronted by a plaza that would become a New York icon in its own right. The center's "front door" is on Fifth Avenue, the stubby Maison Française on the left and mirror-image British Empire edifice on the right. The flower-filled **Channel Gardens** in between provide a route into the heart of the center, culminating in **Rockefeller Plaza.**

Soaring straight up from the plaza, the 70-story **General Electric Building** reflects both the art deco vibe of the 1930s, when most of Rockefeller Center was built, and the boxy modernism of the postwar period. Affectionately called "30 Rock" by those who work within, the skyscraper was originally the home of the Radio Corporation of America (RCA), RKO Pictures, and NBC television. The lobby flaunts massive murals by Spanish artist José

Lee Lawrie's bronze art deco statue of Atlas is Rockefeller Center's largest sculpture, at 45 feet (13.7 m) tall.

Maria Sert, but the real attraction is the **Top of the Rock** observation deck *(tel 212/698-2000, $$$$$, topoftherocknyc.com)* for its expansive views of Manhattan. **Radio City Music Hall** *(tel 212/247-4777, stage door tours: $$$$$, radiocity.com)* is another part of Rockefeller Center worth visiting. With 6,200 seats, it ranks as the largest theater in the United States. The high-kicking Rockettes are among the acts that regularly perform here; behind-the-scenes "stage door" tours are a popular Radio City staple.

Avenue of the Americas between West 48th and 50th Sts.
• tel 212/588-8601 • Subway: B, D, F to 47th-50th Sts.–
Rockefeller Center • rockefellercenter.com

Museum of Modern Art (MoMA)

5 See pp. 96–97.

11 West 53rd St. • tel 212/708-9400 • Closed
Thanksgiving, Dec. 25 • $$$$$ • Subway: E, M to Fifth Ave.–53rd
St or D, F to 47th-50th Sts.–Rockefeller Center • moma.org

St. Patrick's Cathedral

6 The seat of New York's Roman Catholic archdiocese and one of the nation's most renowned churches, St. Patrick's is a tribute to Irish Americans who played such an integral role in New York's history and to the can-do spirit of the 19th-century archbishop John Hughes. Ignoring criticism from wealthy patrons and poor parishioners alike, Hughes launched the project shortly before the Civil War on a patch of land that then lay well outside the city center. Architect James Renwick patterned the massive neo-Gothic structure after Germany's Cologne Cathedral. Although the church was consecrated in 1879, construction continued through the turn of the 20th century. Its twin spires were the tallest landmark along Fifth Avenue until the early 1930s, when skyscrapers overtook

GOOD **EATS**

■ **53**
Located next to MoMA, 53 resembles a gorgeous airport-hanger and serves divine Asian-inspired contemporary fusion dishes. **53 West 53rd St., tel 646/535-3994. $$$$$**

■ **THE OYSTER BAR**
Opened in 1913, this lavishly decorated train-station restaurant serves more than 25 types of oyster and numerous seafood entrees and platters. **Grand Central Terminal, tel 212/490-6650, $$$**

■ **RUSSIAN TEA ROOM**
Founded by members of the exiled Russian Imperial Ballet in 1927, the Tea Room continues as a meeting (and eating) place for local writers, actors, and musicians from nearby Carnegie Hall. **140 West 57th St., tel 212/581-7100, $$**

MIDTOWN NORTH

the neighborhood. The 108-foot-high (34 m) nave can seat 2,500 people, and a number of its exceptionally rich stained-glass windows were made in Chartres, France.

Fifth Ave. between 50th and 51st Sts. • tel 212/753-2261 • Subway: E to Fifth Ave.–53rd St. or 6 to 51st St. • saintpatrickscathedral.org

Grand Central Terminal

7 A masterpiece of beaux arts design, this steel, granite, and limestone building opened in 1913 as the city's state-of-the-art train depot. Outside, beneath the massive central window, a statue commemorates railroad tycoon Cornelius Vanderbilt. In the **Main Concourse,** the vaulted ceiling is decorated with the constellations of the zodiac, and as light streams through cast-iron windows and shadows move across the Tennessee marble floor, the space looks more like an ancient temple than a hub for transportation. The station's culinary offerings include several **gourmet restaurants** and a food court for casual dining.

89 East 42nd St. at Park Ave. • tel 212/340-2583 or 212/532-4900 (train service info) • Subway: 4, 5, 6, 7 to Grand Central–42nd St. • grandcentralterminal.com

Chrysler Building

8 Art deco's fusion of the utilitarian with the artistic reaches its peak in the Chrysler Building. Automobile magnate Walter P. Chrysler funded the structure himself, working closely with architect William Van Alen. Although the 1,050-foot-high (320 m) building kept its "world's tallest" tag for only a year, its artistic merit has continued to soar. Many of Van Alen's architectural details were inspired by car motifs, including the stainless steel gargoyles, modeled after the radiator caps of a 1929 Chrysler. The building is best viewed from the observation deck of the Empire State Building, but visitors can also explore the art deco lobby on weekdays (except public holidays), once a Chrysler showroom.

405 Lexington Ave. • Subway: 4, 5, 6, 7 to Grand Central–42nd St.

The flags of United Nations countries fly in alphabetical order before the Secretariat Building.

United Nations Headquarters

9 A standout along this part of the East River, the building looks as modern today as it did upon its completion in 1952. American architect Wallace K. Harrison had overall design control of the project, but he consulted other maestros, including Brazil's Oscar Niemeyer and Le Corbusier from France, who devised the winning plan. The 39-story **Secretariat Building,** a masterpiece of post-modern skyscraper design, dominates the complex. Directly below is the futuristic **General Assembly** building, with its swayback roof and trademark dome. Guided tours start from the Public Lobby of the General Assembly building. Make time to browse the **gardens** with their river views, as well as diverse examples of modern art, including a 1950s Soviet sculpture, "Let Us Beat Swords into Plowshares," and a bronze monolith by Barbara Hepworth.

First Ave. at 46th St. • Tours: Mon.–Fri. • tel 212/9963-8687 • Closed Sat., Sun., and all major holidays • $$$ • Subway: 4, 5, 6, 7 to 42nd St.–Grand Central • visit.un.org

Museum of Modern Art

MoMA, as it is affectionately known, houses one of the world's leading collections of art from the late 19th century to the present.

The sculpture garden, planted with beech and birch, acts as an outdoor room of the museum.

A few discerning women collectors, including Lillie P. Bliss and Abby Aldrich Rockefeller, founded MoMA in 1929. Today, it holds more than 200,000 pieces of art as well as 22,000 film, video, and media works. The current building opened in 2004, its six floors nearly doubling the exhibition spaces, but the permanent collection still has to be shown in rotating displays. MoMA recently expanded even further, therefore, adding more than 40,000 square feet (3,700 sq m) of new gallery plus performance and experimental art space.

■ The Postimpressionist Era

Highlights in the fifth-floor galleries include Vincent van Gogh's **"The Starry Night,"** painted while the artist was in a mental institution in St. Rémy, France, in 1889. Here, too, you will find Pablo Picasso's 1907 portrait of five prostitutes, **"Les Demoiselles d'Avignon,"** which anticipated cubism.

■ Surrealism & Abstraction

Also on the fifth floor is surrealist Salvador Dalí's masterpiece, **"The Persistence of Memory."** Dalí drew inspiration from an overripe Camembert cheese to depict the melting watches in the painting. In **"Broadway Boogie Woogie,"** Dutch artist Piet Mondrian combined his trademark grid patterning with tiny squares and rectangles of color, suggesting the fast tempo of New York and his interest in jazz.

■ Abstract Expressionism & Pop Art

The fourth floor displays the major figures of abstract expressionism. Jackson Pollock's classic "drip" painting, **"One: Number 31, 1950,"** was created

SAVVY **TRAVELER**

Every floor at MoMA has a space for relaxation. In the central sculpture garden (once the site of founder Abby Aldrich's town house) enjoy a snack among works by Picasso, Auguste Rodin, and others. (See p. 22 for dining options.)

with the canvas laid out on the floor. Latvian-born Mark Rothko painted large, hypnotic canvases composed of rectangles of solid color, such as **"No. 10"** (1950). Pop Art reflected the consumerism of the 1950s and '60s, using the imagery of the mass media, as in Andy Warhol's **"Campbell's Soup Cans"** (1962). Roy Lichtenstein's **"Drowning Girl"** (1963) has the melodrama of a comic strip frame, the speech bubble being part of the picture.

■ Photography

The third-floor collection covers the art form's entire history, including the work of Civil War photographer Matthew Brady. Dorothea Lange made poignant portraits of migrant workers during the 1930s, such as **"Migrant Mother, Nipomo, California."**

11 West 53rd St., between Fifth Ave. and Ave. of the Americas • tel 212/708-9400 • Closed Thanksgiving, Dec. 25 • $$$$$ • Subway: E, M to Fifth Ave.–53rd St. or B, D, F to 47th–50th Sts.–Rockefeller Center • moma.org

MIDTOWN NORTH

Art Deco

The robust lines and soaring spires of the Chrysler and Empire State Buildings were potent symbols of faith in the future, and they epitomize New York's love affair in the 1920s and '30s with the streamlined design of art deco. The style acquired official recognition at a 1925 exhibition in Paris: the "Exposition Internationale des Arts Décoratifs." The shorthand term "art deco" stuck, and the style influenced furniture, textile design, and the applied arts.

The marquetry elevator doors in the Chrysler Building's lobby (above), and its stainless steel stepped spire (right) display art deco style at its most magnificent.

Varied Inspiration

The style drew inspiration from many sources: the ancient civilizations of the Near East, pre-Columbian motifs from the Americas, modern European art movements such as cubism, and contemporary products of the 1920s.

Art deco was extremely versatile. Its sunbursts, chevrons, zigzags, trapezoids, and other geometric patterns could be applied to diners and jewelry, elevators and comic books, planes, trains, and automobiles. Most materials were well suited to its form—from newly invented aluminum and stainless steel to stone, wood, and terra-cotta. Not surprisingly, New York, the city of opportunity, fell for the new style and transformed itself into a science-fiction metropolis of silvery skyscrapers.

Neat Solution

Art deco also solved a problem introduced by the 1916 Zoning Resolution, which required that the niches, shelves, ledges, and rooftops on buildings be "stepped up" to the sky to allow a modicum of sunlight to reach the streets below. Art deco gave these adjustments a decorative purpose, most brilliantly exemplified in the spire of the **Chrysler Building** (see p. 94).

Bold New Look

The **Verizon Building** (previously Barclay-Vesey) at 140 West, designed by Ralph Walker, was the first to represent the bold new look. Completed in 1927, the structure is crowned by a powerful, ornately decorated battlement, and it has ground floor bas-reliefs using the bell motif.

At the 1929 **Chanin Building** (*122 East 42nd St.*), artists Rene Paul Chambellan and Jacques Delamarre decorated the lobby and lower exteriors with bronze, glass, and terra-cotta. The Chrysler Building and **Empire State Building** (see p. 78) also share "high" art deco characteristics of lavishly decorated lobbies and entranceways. **Rockefeller Center** (see pp. 92–93) is another sublime example of the style, with decoration on lower levels, such as the ornate interior of Radio City Music Hall, while Lee Lawrie created superb deco sculptures and bas-reliefs for the public areas.

DECO **SHOPS**

Several notable Manhattan retail buildings exemplify art deco styling.

Bloomingdale's
1000 3rd Ave. at 59th St.
Opened: 1931

Hermès
706 Madison Ave. at East 53rd St.

Tiffany & Co.
6 East 57th St. at Fifth Ave.
Opened: 1940

Christmas

Beginning in late November, the holiday spirit in New York becomes contagious. From 34th Street north along Fifth, Madison, and Third Avenues and around Times Square, the air buzzes with excitement and the streets are laced with glowing lights and the aroma of roasted chestnuts.

■ HOLIDAY WINDOW DISPLAYS

In late November the giant department stores unveil their festive windows. Created by set designers and artists, these mini winterscapes and nostalgic interiors unfold before your eyes, along with whimsical holiday characters and remakes of Christmas movie scenes. The windows at **Macy's** in Midtown South *(151 West 34th St.)* and **Saks Fifth Avenue** *(611 Fifth Ave.)* are the most anticipated; **Lord & Taylor** *(424 Fifth Ave.)*, **Bergdorf Goodman** *(745 Fifth Ave.)*, and **Bloomingdale's** *(1000 Third Ave. at 59th St.)* also join in the fun.

■ CHRISTMAS TREE LIGHTING CEREMONY

Every holiday season, a towering Norway spruce graces **Rockefeller Center** (see pp. 92–93). The tree, which averages about 80 feet (24 m) high, is dressed with more than 5 miles (8 km) of lights and a Swarovski crystal star at the top. At the nationally broadcast lighting ceremony, usually held in late November, a lineup of singers and celebrities launches the festive season with carols and performances, as thousands fill the sidewalks to watch.

■ ICE SKATING

A special delight at this time of year is ice skating. Although many know about the ice rink at **Rockefeller Center** (see pp. 92–93), with its view of the holiday decorations and famous tree, there are other appealing options. Try Central Park's **Wollman Rink** *(59th St. and Fifth Ave., tel 212/439-6900, $$$, wollmanrinknyc.com)*, which offers skating lessons in addition to its magical winter wonderland views. At the park's northern end, the redeveloped **Lasker Rink** will reopen in 2024 *(110th St. and Lenox Ave., tel 212/310-6600, centralpark nyc.org)*. Alternatively, head to

Christmas lights heighten the festive feel at Rockefeller Center's Ice Rink.

The Rink at Bryant Park *(West 42nd St. and Sixth Ave., tel 212/768-4242, skate rental: $$$$, wintervillage.org)* for a charming rink full of good cheer. Admission to the rink is free, and skating lessons are available. Complete your outing with a drink or meal at the Bryant Park Grill restaurant that overlooks the Bryant Park rink.

■ HOLIDAY MARKETS

Pop-up shops and fairs become ubiquitous as shoppers start hunting for the perfect gifts. At **Bryant Park** *(tel 212/768-4242, wintervillage.org)*, you can sip hot chocolate and browse the numerous sparkling booths of the European-style market. The **Grand Central Holiday Fair** *(Grand Central Terminal, grandcentralterminal.com /events)* offers everything from Italian ceramic tableware to handmade hats and scarves. Be sure to check out the light show in the main concourse. The **Holiday Market** at Union Square *(14th St. at Broadway)* pitches festive striped tents full of fun gifts, such as handmade jewelry and old-fashioned toys. The **Holiday Gift Shops** at St. Bartholomew's Church *(325 Park Ave. at 50th St.)* sell cold-weather accessories and handcrafted trinkets.

CARROLL AND
MILTON PETRIE
EUROPEAN
SCULPTURE
COURT

Upper East Side

The Upper East Side, extending from 59th to 110th Streets between Central Park and the East River, has been the neighborhood of choice for the city's wealthy elite since the late 1880s, which accounts for the many town houses, mansions, and upscale shops along the placid blocks from Fifth to Lexington Avenues. From Third Avenue extending east, the scene changes to newer high-rise apartments, although older brownstones can be found on the side streets. Now gentrified, these blocks were once German and Hungarian immigrant neighborhoods, and many of the churches and purveyors here will remind visitors of this heritage. The mayor's official residence, the 18th-century Gracie Mansion, is in Carl Schurz Park along the East River, where a riverside promenade is a peaceful change-of-pace. One stretch of Fifth Avenue has so many museums it is known as Museum Mile. A visitor could spend a week in the Metropolitan Museum of Art alone, so for a day's walk pick the top museums and seek out the key exhibits in each.

◀ **Large works from the 17th to the early 20th centuries grace the European Sculpture Court at the Metropolitan Museum of Art.**

Upper East Side

Early 1900s mansions, fashionable shops, galleries, and museums populate the Upper East Side between Central Park and the East River.

6 Museum of the City of New York

(see p. 110) Dedicated to New York from its earliest days to the present, the museum has an excellent photo archive and period rooms, including John D. Rockefeller's bedroom. Take the 4, 5, or 6 train from 103rd Street to 86th Street, and walk to the end of the street.

5 Jewish Museum

(see p. 109) The former mansion of financier Felix Warburg houses the world's largest collection of Judaica, with many imaginative changing exhibits. Walk up Fifth Avenue to 103rd Street.

4 Solomon R. Guggenheim Museum

(see pp. 107–109) Frank Lloyd Wright's building contains a collection that includes Postimpressionist and abstract works. Continue three blocks up Fifth Avenue

Map labels:

CENTRAL PARK

EAST DRIVE

FIFTH AVENUE

Museum of the City of New York

Jewish Museum

EAST 106TH STREET
EAST 104TH STREET
EAST 103rd Street
EAST 102ND STREET
EAST 96TH STREET
EAST 96th Street

96TH STREET

CARNEGIE HILL

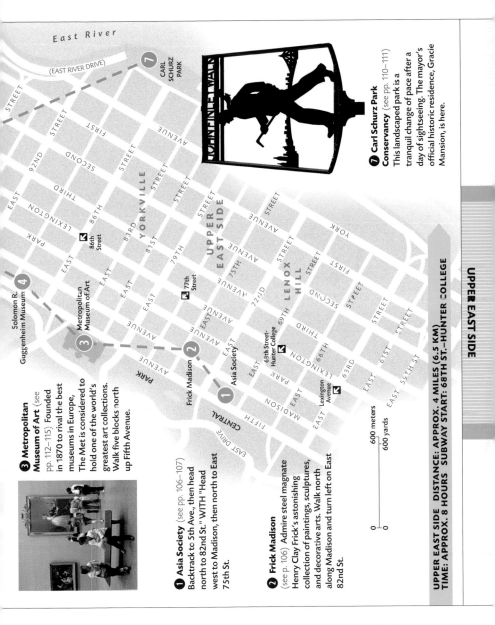

East River

(EAST RIVER DRIVE)

7 CARL SCHURZ PARK

STREET

92ND
STREET

EAST
FIRST
AVENUE

SECOND
STREET

THIRD
STREET

LEXINGTON
86th
Street

PARK
EAST
86TH
STREET

YORKVILLE

STREET

83RD
STREET

4 Solomon R.
Guggenheim Museum

EAST
81ST
STREET

EAST
79TH
STREET

UPPER
EAST
SIDE

3 Metropolitan
Museum of Art

EAST
77th
Street

AVENUE

EAST
75TH
STREET

EAST
72JD
STREET

AVENUE

LENOX
HILL

YORK
AVENUE

FIRST
STREET

SECOND
STREET

2 Frick Madison

PARK
AVENUE

69TH

68th Street
Hunter College

EAST
66TH
STREET

THIRD
STREET

1 Asia Society

EAST
65TH
STREET

LEXINGTON
Lexington
Avenue

63RD
STREET

EAST 61ST STREET

MADISON
EAST 59TH ST

FIFTH

CENTRAL
EAST DRIVE

**7 Carl Schurz Park
Conservancy** (see pp. 110–111)
This landscaped park is a
tranquil change of pace after a
day of sightseeing. The mayor's
official historic residence, Gracie
Mansion, is here.

**3 Metropolitan
Museum of Art** (see
pp. 112–115) Founded
in 1870 to rival the best
museums in Europe,
The Met is considered to
hold one of the world's
greatest art collections.
Walk five blocks north
up Fifth Avenue.

1 Asia Society (see pp. 106–107)
Backtrack to 5th Ave., then head
north to 82nd St." WITH "Head
west to Madison, then north to East
75th St.

2 Frick Madison
(see p. 106) Admire steel magnate
Henry Clay Frick's astonishing
collection of paintings, sculptures,
and decorative arts. Walk north
along Madison and turn left on East
82nd St.

0 ——— 600 meters
0 ——— 600 yards

**UPPER EAST SIDE DISTANCE: APPROX. 4 MILES (6.5 KM)
TIME: APPROX. 8 HOURS SUBWAY START: 68TH ST.–HUNTER COLLEGE**

Asia Society

One of the world's most preeminent organizations devoted to strengthening ties between Asian countries and the United State, the Asia Society was founded in 1956 by John D. Rockefeller III and now includes offices around the world. The crown jewel at the New York headquarters is the Asia Society Museum, whose permanent collection—the **Mr. and Mrs. John D. Rockefeller 3rd Collection**—includes several hundred masterpieces of Asian art dating as far back as the 11th century B.C. Rotating exhibitions are also often on view, with examples from the past including displays of Korean ceramics, Himalayan sculpture, Buddhist art, and Islamic calligraphy. A recent initiative to launch a **Contemporary Art Collection** centered on Asian and Asian-American works has resulted in several exciting additions to the collection focused on video, animation, and new media works of art. Featured artists include Yoko Ono, Patty Chang, and Xu Bing. The collection also showcases the work of contemporary photographers, among them Hong Lei and Zhang Dali. There are reasons to come after hours, too: The Asia Society hosts regular evening events ranging from panel discussions to film screenings and concerts.

725 Park Avenue at 70th St. • tel 212/288-6400 • Closed Mon. • $$$ • Subway: 6 to 68th St./Hunter College or F to 63rd St. Lexington Avenue. • asiasociety.org

A visitor contemplates Paolo Veronese's "Wisdom and Strength" at the Frick.

The Frick Collection

The mansion that steel magnate Henry Clay Frick (1849–1919) commissioned from the prestigious Carrère and Hastings architecture firm presents a rare opportunity to appreciate art in an intimate residential setting. Frick filled his home, completed in 1914, with 18th-century French furniture and porcelain, Oriental rugs, paintings, and sculpture, including an exceptional assortment of small bronzes, with paintings arranged randomly, much as they were when Frick lived here. In 2021, the collection was transferred to **Frick Madison** (*945 Madison Ave.*), the institution's temporary home five blocks away, while the historic Frick mansion, with its skylit **Garden Court** (an oasis of greenery), receives a more energy-efficient refurbishment through 2024. Here, works are organized chronologically and by region. Impressive decorative arts include seventeenth-century Mughal carpets alongside treasured paintings and sculptures by El Greco, Gainsborough, Goya, Holbein, Manet, Rembrandt, Titian, Turner, van Dyck, Velázquez, Vermeer, Whistler, and many others. Important works include a late "**Self Portrait**" by Rembrandt, Diego Velázquez's "**King Philip IV of Spain**," Jean-Honoré Fragonard's playful series "**The Progress of Love**," and Johannes Vermeer's "**Mistress and Maid**," "**Girl Interrupted at Her Music**," and "**Officer and Laughing Girl**"— tracing Frick's interest in this enigmatic artist.

1 East 70th St. at Fifth Ave. • tel 212/288-0700 • Closed Mon. and major holidays • $$$$ • Subway: 6 to 68th St.–Hunter College • frick.org

Metropolitan Museum of Art
3 See pp. 112–115.

1000 Fifth Avenue at 82nd St. • tel 212/535-7710 • Closed Wed. (except holidays), Jan. 1, Thanksgiving, Dec. 25 • $$$$$ • Subway: 4, 5, 6 to 86th St. • metmuseum.org

Solomon R. Guggenheim Museum
4 Without question, the Guggenheim's most famous exhibit is its own landmark building by the American architect Frank Lloyd Wright, as stunningly modernistic today as when it was completed in 1959. Wright's spiraling ramps show off art as few settings can. Exhibits have featured everything from master works to motorcycles. The permanent collection began with

businessman and benefactor Solomon R. Guggenheim's own store of 600 "non-objective paintings" by abstract artists, such as Vassily Kandinsky and Rudolf Bauer. Forming part of this core collection are Kandinsky's **"Composition 8"** and Bauer's **"Invention (Composition 31)."** Guggenheim also sought out early pioneers of modern art with highly distinctive figurative styles. Examples include Amedeo Modigliani's **"Nude,"** Franz Marc's **"Yellow Cow,"** and Marc Chagall's **"Green Violinist."** A series of donations and purchases has since enriched the museum's holdings; the Justin K. Thannhauser bequest, for instance, added Impressionist and Postimpressionist masterpieces. Don't miss Paul Cézanne's **"Still Life: Flask, Glass, and Jug,"** Vincent van Gogh's **"Mountains at Saint-Rémy,"** and Pablo Picasso's **"Woman with Yellow Hair."** Other important acquisitions include works by Joan Miró and Paul Klee, and minimalist, postminimalist, environmental, and

The Rotunda at the Guggenheim gives access to additional galleries in the adjoining Annex.

conceptual work by contemporary artists such as Doris Salcedo, Mona Hatoum, and Sarah Sze. The Thannhauser collection is on permanent view, while a donation by The Robert Mapplethorpe Foundation of 200 photographs usually appears as part of themed exhibits. Take the elevator to the top of the Rotunda and view the collections as you descend the gently sloping ramp.

1071 Fifth Ave. at 89th St. • tel 212/423-3500 • Closed Tue., Thanksgiving, and Dec. 25 • $$$$$ • Subway: 4, 5, 6 to 86th St. • guggenheim.org

Jewish Museum

5 This impressive museum, founded in 1904, chronicles the diversity of Jewish culture, both religious and secular. The French Gothic–style mansion of philanthropist Felix Warburg has housed the collections since 1947. It has been twice expanded and a sculpture court added to accommodate the vast holdings. These include nearly 30,000 objects that encompass paintings, sculpture, photography, archaeological artifacts, and ceremonial objects. A two-floor permanent exhibit, **"Culture and Continuity: The Jewish Journey,"** explores Jewish history through art, artifacts, video, photos, and TV excerpts, following the Jewish experience over 4,000 years, through harsh and tragic circumstances. Art here includes works by Elie Nadelman, Ben Shahn, Ross Bleckner, and Alfred Stieglitz. The museum also hosts temporary exhibits that have ranged from Paris salons to the Dead Sea Scrolls and celebrated Jewish luminaries in the arts.

1109 Fifth Ave. at 92nd St. • tel 212/423-3200 • Closed Tue. and Wed. • $$$$, free on Jewish holidays • Subway: 4, 5, 6 to 86th St. or 96th St. • thejewishmuseum.org

GOOD **EATS**

■ **DANIEL**
Daniel Boulud's very elegant home base is considered one of the city's finest restaurants. **60 East 65th St., tel 212/288-0033, $$$$**

■ **DAVID BURKE TAVERN**
Taking up two stories in a historic townhouse, celebrity-chef David Burke's upscale temple to health-conscious contemporary American fare. **135 East 62nd St., tel 212/754-1300, $$-$$$$**

■ **MISSION CEVICHE**
This gourmet restaurant specializes in classic Peruvian dishes. Chef José Luis Chávez's ceviches steal the show. **1400 2nd Ave., tel 212/650-0014, $$**

■ **PASTRAMI QUEEN**
Dressed with grainy mustard or Russian dressing, the pastrami rye and corned beef sandwiches are among New York's finest. **1125 Lexington Ave., tel 212/734-1500, $-$$**

UPPER EAST SIDE

Museum of the City of New York

6 The collections here got their start in 1923 as a small exhibit in Gracie Mansion (see opposite). This proved so popular that a Fifth Avenue site was found for a full-scale museum dedicated to New York's history and heritage. For a comprehensive understanding of New York, begin with **Timescapes,** a 22-minute multimedia experience, narrated by actor Stanley Tucci, that traces the city's growth from a settlement of a few hundred Europeans, Africans, and Native Americans to one of the world's great metropolises. Also on permanent view is the **Theater Collection,** which documents theatrical performance in New York City from 1785 to contemporary Broadway productions, bolstered by objects and memorabilia on such popular entertainment as burlesque, vaudeville, and circus. The museum's enormous collections comprise some 750,000 objects, including paintings, photographs, and prints, as well as the photography collections of Jacob Riis and Berenice Abbott, and more than 3,000 prints by the 19th-century printmaking firm of Currier & Ives. A menu of special exhibits completes the museum's attractions, which have benefited from a multimillion-dollar expansion adding three floors of gallery space.

SAVVY **TRAVELER**

The 92nd Street Y (*1395 Lexington Ave. at 92nd St., tel 212/415-5500***) is one of the city's cultural hubs, home to a steady schedule of dance, music, poetry readings, and talks on politics and the arts.**

1220 Fifth Ave. at 103rd St. • tel 212/534-1672 • Closed Tues., Wed., and Jan. 1, Thanksgiving, Dec. 25 • $$$$ • Subway: 6 to 103rd St. or 2,3 to Central Park North–110th St. • mcny.org

Carl Schurz Park Conservancy

7 This hilly park spanning 15.2 acres (6.2 ha) overlooks the racing waters of the East River, at a section known as Hell Gate, where it meets the Harlem River and Long Island Sound. Stroll around the park to see the landscaping with ornamental stairs and lovely plantings, stretch your legs on the 10-block walkway along the river above East River Drive, or sit on a bench to contemplate the view. In 1798, Archibald Gracie (1755–1829), a Scottish-born shipping magnate, bought property here for a country retreat, and he built his elegant mansion the following year. His parties were attended by such illustrious guests as President John Quincy Adams and future French king Louis-Philippe. In 1891, the city acquired the former Gracie estate, amalgamating it with the adjoining East River Park. The last of the country mansions that once lined Manhattan's East River shore, and one of Manhattan's oldest surviving wood structures, **Gracie Mansion** was the first home of the Museum of the City of New York and has served as the official residence of New York's mayors since 1942, when Fiorello La Guardia moved here. Guided tours of the antique-filled mansion are given every Monday at 10:30 a.m. and 2 p.m. The park was named in 1910 for the German-born soldier, statesman, and journalist Carl Schurz (1829–1906).

East End Ave. at East 86th St. • Subway: 4, 5, 6 to 86th St. • carlschurzparknyc.org•
Gracie Mansion: East End Ave. at East 88th St. • tel 212/570-4751 • $$ • graciemansion.org

Gracie Mansion, New York's oldest wooden building, is a model of early American style.

Metropolitan Museum of Art

The largest art collection in the U.S., The Met can be overwhelming so decide what to see before you go.

The Met has stood on its current site in Central Park since 1880.

At the Metropolitan Museum of Art, ancient Mesopotamia, 19th-century Paris, and 1960s New York are just yards and minutes away from each other. Founded in 1870 with the mission of collecting and exhibiting works that represent the "broadest spectrum of human achievement at the highest level of quality," The Met is one of the world's premier encyclopedic art museums. The sprawling galleries, spanning four city blocks, feature a collection drawn from six continents and covering eight millennia of world history.

■ Ancient Egypt
The first-floor Egyptian collection includes art and artifacts from the Old Kingdom to the era of Roman rule. Everyday objects appear alongside elaborate artwork made for the pharaohs and are a window into life along the Nile over thousands of years. Wood-carved models from **Meketre's Tomb,** circa 2000 B.C., function like miniature dioramas showing how this Theban official's estate operated and made him wealthy.

■ Greek & Roman Art
Beginning before the Geometric Period (900–700 B.C.) and ending in the Hellenistic (323–31 B.C.), this collection on the first floor comprises sculpture, glass, pottery, and wall painting. Among the stars is a beautifully painted **amphora** (two-handled jar) by the sixth-century B.C. Athenian potter and vase-painter Exekias. It shows four horses drawing a wedding chariot.

■ European Art
A meander around the first and second floors takes visitors from Renaissance Italy to Rembrandt's Amsterdam to van Gogh's adopted home in the south of France. Even in such distinguished company as this, there are standouts.

Pieter Brueghel the Elder's **"The Harvesters"** (1565), depicting wheatfields and peasants, is one of the first major paintings on a secular rather than religious theme. Diego Velázquez's **"Juan de Pareja"** is one of his few paintings of a non-royal subject.

■ Modern Art
The Lila Acheson Wallace Wing houses The Met's growing collection of modern art. Major works by modernist superstars include Pablo Picasso's **"Portrait of Gertrude Stein,"** Jackson Pollock's **"Autumn Rhythm (Number 30),"** and Constantin Brâncuşi's **"Bird in Space."** Among the slightly lesser-known pieces are Romare Bearden's **"The Block"** (1971)—a collage depicting life in Harlem—and Marsden Hartley's **"Portrait of a German Officer"** (1914), created from metals, badges, and banners.

UPPER EAST SIDE

■ TEMPLE OF DENDUR

In Gallery 131, intact temple, circa 15 B.C., from southern Egypt, is dedicated to the goddess Isis and two local deities. Wall carvings show the pharoah making offerings to the gods. The temple was built when Egypt was under Roman control, so the pharaoh depicted is actually Caesar Augustus.

■ JOHN VANDERLYN PANORAMA

Painted panoramas became popular attractions in the United States in the 19th century. They were designed to surround the viewer, who had the feeling of standing in the location depicted. John Vanderlyn's circular painting of **Versailles,** in the American Wing on the first floor, transports visitors to a spot in the middle of the royal French gardens, surrounded by elaborate fountains, manicured hedgerows, and strutting monarchs.

■ GUBBIO STUDIOLO

Designed ca **1479–1482** for Federico da Montefeltro, duke of Urbino, the *studiolo* (study) is a triumph in woodworking, on view in Gallery 501 on the first floor. The duke used

The Temple of Dendur once stood on the Nile, represented by a reflecting pool.

it as a personal haven in his palace at Gubbio, where he could study and think in peace. Using only wood inlay, the maker of this small room created a space lined with trompe l'oeil bookshelves and cabinets. He filled the shelves with the duke's favorite books, musical instruments, and scientific tools, also in wood inlay.

■ ROMAN CUBICULUM
The colorful *cubiculum* (Latin for bedroom) in Gallery 165 on the first floor comes from a place near Pompeii in Italy. Painted ca 50–40 B C, the **frescoes** show deities, altars with offerings to the gods, and objects such as trompe l'oeil glass vases. The eruption of Vesuvius in A.D. 79 buried the cubiculum in lava and ash, preserving the frescoes until they were excavated in the early 20th century.

■ ASTOR COURT
This indoor garden, installed in the second-floor Asian galleries, was built by a team of Chinese craftsmen in the early 1980s. They modeled it on a Ming Dynasty (1368–1644) scholar's garden. You enter through a moon gate (circular doorway) and continue

DON'T **MISS**

Millionaire Robert Lehman left a superb collection of works by Rembrandt, El Greco, and other great artists to The Met. See this often-missed area on the first floor in the Lehman Wing.

along a covered walkway. In one corner a small koi pond is surrounded by authentic Chinese *taihu* rocks— craggy, pockmarked limestone rocks that are prized elements of a scholar's garden. The Astor Court is always tranquil, a good place to pause during a day at The Met.

■ FRANK LLOYD WRIGHT ROOM
The American Period Rooms on the third floor include this living room by the 20th-century Chicago architect. Wright also designed and built the house it belonged to in a Minneapolis suburb around 1913. His signature features include low overhanging roofs and windows with geometric designs. The room was conceived in relation to the rural location of the house, and to evoke this original wooded setting, the museum installed the room so that it overlooks Central Park.

UPPER EAST SIDE

1000 Fifth Avenue at 82nd St. • tel 212/535-7710 • Closed Wed. (except holidays), Jan. 1, Thanksgiving, Dec. 25, and first Monday in May • $$$$$ • Subway: 4, 5, 6 to 86th St. • metmuseum.org

Gallery Hopping

New York's galleries are the most exciting in the United States. The city, which has long attracted many of the world's leading artists, is the focal point of the nation's art market as well as a major center of the international contemporary art world. Hundreds of New York galleries represent a huge range of artists, from established stars to the latest iconoclasts. The gallery scene is often a moveable feast, tending to follow the paths of artists.

Tom Otterness's "Mama Bear" (above) was shown by Marlborough Gallery at the 2011 Armory Show. Opposite: Works from Pieter Schoolwerth's exhibition entitled "Your Vacuum Blows, which Sucks" at the Miguel Abreu Gallery

Around Midtown

After the Museum of Modern Art opened on West 53rd Street in 1929, the first cluster of important galleries appeared nearby on the upper floors of buildings around 57th Street. Early galleries, such as Peggy Guggenheim's Art of This Century, were the first to showcase the works of painters of the New York school, who included Jackson Pollock and Mark Rothko. Today's 57th Street still has prestigious contemporary galleries, such as **Marian Goodman** (*24 West 57th St.*), representing Steve McQueen and Gerhard Richter, and **Alexandre Gallery** (*25 East 73rd St.*), with Ann Arnold and Edith Schloss.

Chelsea & the Lower East Side

In the 1990s, art dealers began to eye the lofty, low-rent spaces of Chelsea, running from West 18th to 27th Streets, between 10th and 11th Avenues. Until then, gas stations, garages, and warehouses were the area's main features. Now some 300 galleries line the streets or stack up in

UPPER EAST SIDE

vertical "art malls"—buildings where the elevator opens to a different showroom on every floor. Chelsea is all about the avant-garde; its leading names include **Matthew Marks** *(523 West 24th St.)*, **Luhring Augustine** *(531 West 24th St.)*, **Gladstone Gallery** *(515 West 24th Street)*, and **Gagosian** *(555 West 24th St.)*.

Another burgeoning area is the Lower East Side. In 2010, **Sperone Westwater** *(257 Bowery)* moved here from Chelsea, signaling the area's emergence as an art mecca. The gallery represents artists such as Bruce Nauman, Tom Sachs, and William Wegman. The experimental **Miguel Abreu Gallery** *(36 Orchard St. and 88 Eldridge St.)* represents Liz Deschenes, Sam Lewitt, and Pieter Schoolwerth, among other artists.

THE **ARMORY SHOW**

The legendary 1913 Armory Show in New York City introduced European modern art that both shocked the public and influenced art making and collecting in the U.S. New York continues to attract important shows, including a modern version of the Armory Show each year.

Javits Center, One Penn Plaza, tel 212/645-6440, thearmoryshow.com

Upper East Side Shops

The Upper East Side lures visitors with some of New York's most exciting shopping, from upscale designer boutiques to world-famous department stores, and books, accessories, gifts, and more in the many museum shops. Some of the price tags may be steep, but browsing is absolutely free.

■ DEPARTMENT STORES

Bloomingdale's (*1000 Third Ave. at East 59th St.*) is rightfully famed as a trendsetter, its seven floors overflowing with the latest creations from famous label designers for men and women, as well as fine selections of cosmetics, housewares, gourmet foods, electronics, luggage, linens, and furniture. Two blocks away, ultra-chic, ultra-mod, ultra-expensive **Saks Fifth Avenue** (*611 Fifth Ave.*) prides itself on exclusive and avant-garde fashions and accessories. Its inimitable style also extends to home accessories and cosmetics.

SAVVY **TRAVELER**

The French menu at L'Avenue at **Saks Fifth Avenue** (*tel 212/753-4000, $$$*) is a favorite with sophisticated shoppers. At Bloomingdale's **Le Train Bleu** (*tel 212/705-2100, $$$*), French dishes are served in the atmospheric setting of a Parisian train car.

■ MADISON AVENUE

The upscale blocks from 60th to 79th Streets on Madison Avenue are packed with shops featuring the world's top designers. A sampling of the long and distinguished list runs: **Tom Ford** (*No. 672*); **Missoni** (*No. 676*); **Giorgio Armani** (*No. 761*); **Michael Kors** (*No. 790*); **Carolina Herrera** (*No. 802*); **Lanvin** (*No. 849*); **Valentino** (*No. 821*); **Dolce & Gabbana** (*No. 827*); **Asprey** (*No. 678*); and **Ralph Lauren,** with two fashion castles at (*No. 867*) and (*No. 888*). Other luxury names include: **Bottega Veneta** (*No. 740*) for shoes and leather goods; **Frette** (*No. 799*) for fine linens; **Vera Wang** (*No. 991*), if you see a bridal gown in your future; **Christofle** (*41 East 57th St., on the corner of Madison Ave.*) for French crystal, china, and silver; and **Victoria's Secret** (*640 5th Ave., one block from Madison Ave.*) for

The Victoria's Secret store on Broadway in the Soho area of downtown Manhattan

lingerie. Jewelry shoppers with bulging bank accounts should investigate the stores around 66th and 67th Streets for **Fred Leighton** *(No. 773)*, **David Webb** *(No. 942)*, and **Breguet** *(699 5th Ave., one block from Madison Ave.)*.

■ MUSEUM SHOPS

All the Upper East Side museums have shops with distinctive wares, but three are exceptional. Besides art posters and a huge array of books, the expansive shopping area at the **Metropolitan Museum of Art** (see pp. 112–115) has everything from jewelry and scarves to stationery and home décor, all in delightful taste. At the **Jewish Museum** (see p. 109) you can peruse quality china, candlesticks, frames, jewelry, and toys, many at reasonable prices. For a fine display of illustrated books and other appealing items, all with a New York City theme (including a LEGO model of the Rockefeller Center), there's no better place than the shop on the first floor at the **Museum of the City of New York** (see p. 110).

Central Park

Journalist Frederick Law Olmsted and architect Calvert Vaux designed the country's first landscaped park in 1858 to meet a need for urban greenery. In the 19th century, as ordinary New Yorkers searched for respite from the city, members of high society began pressing for a dedicated public space in which to socialize, and where the lower classes would benefit from fresh air. After a lengthy debate, an area of Manhattan unsuitable for commercial buildings was chosen as the site of the new park. Twenty thousand workers spent 20 years turning swamps into lakes, redesigning the rocky landscape, planting more than 270,000 trees and shrubs, and transforming the whole area into an idyllic pastoral oasis. Central Park (centralparknyc.org) stretches south to north from 59th Street to 110th Street and across from Fifth Avenue to Central Park West. The land on which it stands is estimated to be worth more than $200 billion. Inside the park you can swim, ice skate, go boating, cycle, walk, or just enjoy the many lovely gardens.

◀ Seen from above, the park's 843 acres (341 ha) form a vast verdant area—a stark contrast to the density of the skyscrapers that surround it.

Central Park

Among the attractions in the city's premier green space are gardens, lakes, a Gothic castle, and a memorial to former Beatle John Lennon.

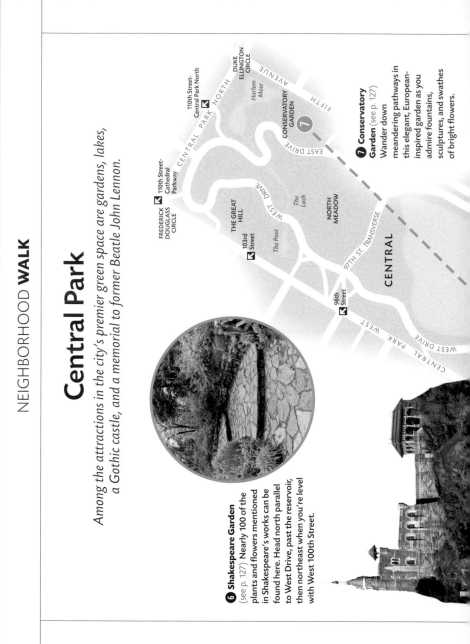

6 Shakespeare Garden
(see p. 127) Nearly 100 of the plants and flowers mentioned in Shakespeare's works can be found here. Head north parallel to West Drive, past the reservoir, then northeast when you're level with West 100th Street.

7 Conservatory Garden (see p. 127) Wander down meandering pathways in this elegant, European-inspired garden as you admire fountains, sculptures, and swathes of bright flowers.

110th Street-Central Park North

DUKE ELLINGTON CIRCLE

Harlem Meer

CENTRAL PARK NORTH

FIFTH AVENUE

CONSERVATORY GARDEN

FREDERICK DOUGLASS CIRCLE

110th Street-Cathedral Parkway

EAST DRIVE

THE GREAT HILL

103rd Street

The Loch

The Pool

WEST DRIVE

NORTH MEADOW

97TH ST. TRANSVERSE

96th Street

CENTRAL

CENTRAL PARK WEST

WEST DRIVE

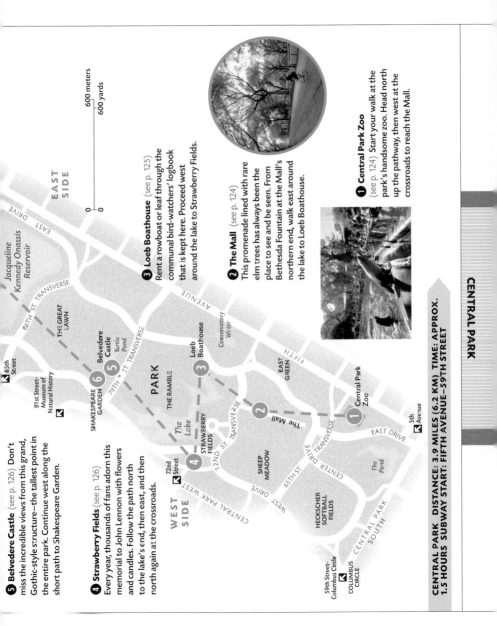

5 Belvedere Castle (see p. 126) Don't miss the incredible views from this grand, Gothic-style structure—the tallest point in the entire park. Continue west along the short path to Shakespeare Garden.

4 Strawberry Fields (see p. 126) Every year, thousands of fans adorn this memorial to John Lennon with flowers and candles. Follow the path north to the lake's end, and then east, and then north again at the crossroads.

3 Loeb Boathouse (see p. 125) Rent a rowboat or leaf through the communal bird-watchers' logbook that is kept here. Proceed west around the lake to Strawberry Fields.

2 The Mall (see p. 124) This promenade lined with rare elm trees has always been the place to see and be seen. From Bethesda Fountain at the Mall's northern end, walk east around the lake to Loeb Boathouse.

1 Central Park Zoo (see p. 124) Start your walk at the park's handsome zoo. Head north up the pathway, then west at the crossroads to reach the Mall.

600 meters
600 yards
0
0

Jacqueline Kennedy Onassis Reservoir

EAST SIDE

EAST DRIVE

86th Street

85th Street

THE GREAT LAWN

81st Street–Museum of Natural History

SHAKESPEARE GARDEN

6

5 Belvedere Castle

Turtle Pond

79TH ST. TRANSVERSE

PARK

THE RAMBLE

3 Loeb Boathouse

Conservatory Water

FIFTH AVENUE

The Lake

72nd Street

4

STRAWBERRY FIELDS

72ND ST. TRANSVERSE

WEST SIDE

CENTRAL PARK WEST

2 The Mall

EAST GREEN

EAST DRIVE

5th Avenue

1 Central Park Zoo

SHEEP MEADOW

65TH ST. TRANSVERSE

CENTER DRIVE

The Pond

HECKSCHER SOFTBALL FIELDS

WEST DRIVE

CENTRAL PARK SOUTH

59th Street–Columbus Circle

COLUMBUS CIRCLE

CENTRAL PARK DISTANCE: 3.9 MILES (6.2 KM) TIME: APPROX. 1.5 HOURS SUBWAY START: FIFTH AVENUE–59TH STREET

CENTRAL PARK

Central Park Zoo

1 More than 150 species from around the world live in the Central Park Zoo, including red pandas, grizzly bears, and rare snow leopards. The modern five-acre (2 ha) facility was first established as a makeshift menagerie in 1860, expanded in the 1930s, and refurbished in 1984. Among its highlights are the octagonal sea lion pool in the central courtyard, where daily feedings take place, and the **Tisch Children's Zoo,** where kids get the chance to pet and feed goats, alpacas, Vietnamese pot-bellied pigs, and more. Preservationists will delight at seeing the limestone friezes of birds, monkeys, and lions—vestiges of the 1930s-era zoo that was built to replace the menagerie. The **Delacorte Clock** will enchant all with its parade of brass animals circling to the tunes of nursery rhymes every half-hour.

Fifth Ave. and 64th St. • tel 212/439-6500 • $$$$ • Subway: N, Q, R to 59th St.–5th Ave. • centralparkzoo.com

The Mall

2 This long, tree-lined pedestrian walkway is the spot where New Yorkers used to come to stroll in their Sunday best, and it is still a great place for people-watching. It is flanked by benches and rows of giant American elms forming a leafy canopy, enticing many photographers into trying to capture the perfect Central Park shot. Not only visually stunning, the Mall's majestic trees also form one of the largest remaining collections of American elms in the country; the rest of the population has been nearly wiped out by Dutch elm disease. **Literary Walk,** at the southern end of the promenade, displays five bronze statues of famous writers, including William Shakespeare and Scottish poet Robert Burns; the other end of the walkway culminates at **Bethesda Terrace,** an ornately carved overlook with views of the lake and the wooded Ramble beyond.

Mid-park from 66th to 72nd Sts. • Subway: B, C to 72nd St.

Loeb Boathouse

③ The lake's eastern tip is graced by the elegant Loeb Boathouse. The large, copper-roofed, redbrick building opened in 1954, replacing a Victorian boathouse designed in 1874 by Calvert Vaux. You can rent bicycles to tour the park from here, and rowboats and Venetian gondolas (complete with singing gondoliers) to glide across the 18-acre (7.2 ha) lake. For the city's bird-watchers, the boathouse is significant for a different reason, namely a communally written notebook detailing all bird sightings in the park, updated by enthusiasts almost every day. If you're an avid ornithologist, peruse the notebook and record your observations. The Boathouse, which appeared in such movies as *The Manchurian Candidate* and *When Harry Met Sally,* was one of New York's most iconic restaurants until closing in October 2022.

East side between 74th and 75th Sts. • tel 212/517-2233 • Boat rentals: $$$ • thecentralparkboathouse.com

People navigate the water on boats in Central Park

Strawberry Fields

4 The memorial to musician and songwriter John Lennon is a 2.5-acre (1 ha), tear-shaped garden across the street from **The Dakota** building (see pp. 136–137), where Lennon and his wife, Yoko Ono, lived at the time of his murder in 1980. The couple often visited this peaceful stretch of the park, which today attracts thousands of fans on the anniversaries of Lennon's birth (October 9) and death (December 8), with many staying late into the night singing their favorite songs. A black-and-white mosaic on the ground with the word "Imagine" marks the heart of the memorial, and a nearby bronze plaque lists the 121 countries that have donated trees, plants, and stones to endorse the site as a garden of peace. Many fans leave flowers, candles, and other gifts in tribute to the legendary Beatle.

Central Park West, between 72nd and 73rd Sts. • Subway: B, C to 72nd St.

GOOD **EATS**

■ **TAVERN ON THE GREEN**
IIt has a seasonal menu, but it's the woodsy open-air dining that makes this restaurant a favorite with New Yorkers.
67th St. and Central Park West, tel 212/877-8684, $$$$

■ **CAFÉ SABARSKY**
This Viennese standout in the Neue Galerie is known for its excellent goulash, sausages, strudels, and tortes.
1048 Fifth Ave. and 88th St., tel 212/288-0665, $$$

■ **PASTRAMI QUEEN**
Near Strawberry Fields, this kosher deli rivals Katz's for its pastrami sandwiches and matzo ball soup.
138 West 72nd St., tel 212/734-1500, $$

Belvedere Castle

5 Standing at the highest point in the park, Belvedere Castle offers panoramic views of both greenery and cityscapes from its granite towers. When it was built in 1869, it was intended as a whimsical lookout. The National Weather Service has been taking the city's temperature from here every day since 1919. The castle also attracts nature enthusiasts: children can borrow a **Discovery Kit** backpack containing binoculars, a guidebook, a map, and sketching materials for free; and everyone can enjoy events, including the **"On A Wing"** series, which explores Central Park's many winged creatures.

Mid-park at 79th St. • tel 332/213-3947 • Closed Mon.-Tue., Jan. 1, Thanksgiving, Dec. 25 • Subway: B, C to 81st St.

Shakespeare Garden

6 Literature lovers should not miss Shakespeare Garden. The quiet, 4-acre (1.6 ha) spread abounds with many of the plants mentioned in Shakespeare's poems and plays, including the distinctly Elizabethan-sounding flax and cowslip, primrose, wormwood, quince, and lark's heel. Beautifully landscaped and secluded, with a twisting, ascending path dotted with rustic wooden benches and bronze plaques inscribed with quotations from the Bard, the garden is a hidden gem. Highlights include an enchanting stone staircase built into a steep slope, the **Swedish Cottage**—literally transported from Sweden in 1877 and now home to a marionette theater—and a mulberry tree that some believe was grown from a cutting taken in Shakespeare's mother's garden in Stratford-upon-Avon, England. The garden is especially spectacular in spring, when crocuses, hyacinths, and roses are in bloom.

West side, between 79th and 80th Sts. • Subway: B, C to 72nd St.

Conservatory Garden

7 This 6-acre (2.4 ha) garden is a popular spot for weddings, thanks to its fairy-tale like setting. It is composed of three distinct sections: Italian, French, and English. The central, Italian-style garden is a large lawn, bordered by two pink-and-white crabtree allées. The French-inspired garden is bursting with color when tulips bloom in spring and in fall when chrysanthemums put on their annual show. Circular pathways meander around the English-style garden, as magnolias and Japanese lilac trees perfume the air in spring and summer. A project of restoration currently in progress is expected to be completed by late 2024.

During spring in the French-inspired garden, tulips bloom behind the Untermayer Fountain.

East side, between 104th St. and 106th St. • Subway: 6 to 103rd St.

The City's the Star

New York's towering buildings, hectic streets, and colorful characters have inspired many filmmakers since the 1890s, with some of America's best-loved movies set here. More than 200 films feature scenes that have been set in Central Park alone, from the sinister assault on Dustin Hoffman and his girlfriend in *Marathon Man* to the task-force-type penguins digging a tunnel to escape from the Central Park Zoo in *Madagascar.*

Next Stop, Greenwich Village **was among several movies to feature Caffe Reggio (above). Audrey Hepburn attracted large crowds while filming the opening shots of** *Breakfast at Tiffany's* **(right).**

Early Days

Although New York was first captured on the silver screen in William Heise's motion picture *Herald Square* (1896), many subsequent movies set in Manhattan were shot on California sets—such as Alfred Hitchcock's *Rear Window* in 1954. This changed with the 1960s "New Hollywood" film era, when filmmakers such as Martin Scorsese, Francis Ford Coppola, and Woody Allen created commercial and critical success with stories revolving around, and shot in, New York.

Downtown Realism

New York's Lower East Side is one of the city's oldest neighborhoods, with a rich history of immigrant culture. Coppola and Gordon Parks found inspiration here, though Greenwich Village's **Caffe Reggio** (see p. 65) appears as a backdrop in their gritty films, *The Godfather Part II* and *Shaft*. Farther south, **Little Italy**'s roads provided the ideal location for Scorcese's seedy, hard-hitting classics *Mean Streets* and *Taxi Driver*.

Uptown Charm

When Audrey Hepburn gazed into the window of **Tiffany & Co.,** she forever cemented Fifth Avenue's glamorous reputation. Farther up the avenue is the elegant **Plaza** hotel (see p. 183), home to Eloise from the eponymous children's books and movie, and the spot where a fictional young guest played by Macaulay Culkin racked up a thousand-dollar room service bill in *Home Alone II*.

Love Is in the Air

Numerous sites feature in the city's romances. Rising above them all is the **Empire State Building** (see p. 78), scene of the emotional climaxes that brought *Sleepless in Seattle* and *An Affair to Remember* to a memorable close.

TV **TOURS**

Follow in the footsteps of your favorite TV characters on a guided tour based on famous shows. You'll visit spots such as the apartment building used in *Friends*, Aidan's Scout Bar from *Sex and the City*, *Gossip Girl*'s school, and, of course, *The Sopranos'* Bada Bing nightclub. While on these tours you can eat, drink, and shop just like your favorite stars.

onlocationtours.com, tel 212/683-2027, $$$$$

Outdoor Activities

New York may be a concrete jungle, but there is plenty to do in the great outdoors. Join the cyclists and runners on the city's many miles of greenway. Take a relaxing summer swim in an outdoor pool, and you can even kayak on the Hudson River and get a fresh angle on the city experience.

CENTRAL PARK

■ BIKING

New York City opened the country's first bike path in 1894 and now has more than 250 miles (402 km) of cycling paths, many of them in Central Park. **Bikerent.nyc** has rental shops at various locations *(tel 212/541-8759, $$$-$$$$, bikerent.nyc)*. The **Manhattan Waterfront Greenway,** which circumnavigates the island, is a 32-mile (51.5 km) traffic-free path for runners and cyclists. (To get there, ride west from Central Park directly to the Hudson River.) Most rentals include a helmet, basket, lock, and map. Stop for stop signs and red lights or face a fine.

Bikes can be rented from Bike Rental Central Park (1391 6th Ave., tel 212/664-9600, bikerentalcentralpark.com).

■ RUNNING

Central Park has lanes dedicated to running as well as biking. Every lamp post on the Central Park Loop—the

6-mile (9.6 km) interior road that encircles the park—is marked with a street number and a W (west) or E (east), so you cannot get lost easily. If you would prefer to run on the streets, keeping track of your mileage is easy: Every 20 blocks north-south is one mile (1.6 km). A memorable way to see Manhattan is from the waterfront, so try running along any stretch of the **Greenway**—most spots offer excellent views. You'll pass parks, harbors, and gardens, and see the **Statue of Liberty** (see pp. 50–51) and other city landmarks along the way.

centralparknyc.org

■ KAYAKING

The all-volunteer crews at **Downtown Boathouse** and **Manhattan Community Boathouse** offer kayaking lessons for all levels with colorful, sit-on-top plastic kayaks.

It's polite to run counterclockwise around Central Park's lake.

It's perfect for children and beginners, who can safely play on the Hudson and explore the river. Best of all, it's free.

Downtown Boathouse: Pier 26 (near Hubert St.), open weekends and holidays May–Oct., downtownboathouse.org; Manhattan Community Boathouse: Pier 96 (Hudson River Park at 56th St.) and 72nd St., open weekends May–Oct., manhattancommunityboathouse.org

■ SWIMMING

New York City has plenty of outdoor public swimming pools. Central Park's **Lasker Pool** (*open June to Labor Day*), in the northeast corner at 106th Street, is free; currently being renovated, it will reopen in 2024. If you don't want

to go when the city's children are splashing around, aim for a lap swim (*tel 212/565-8687, call for schedules*). Bring your own lock, towel, bathing cap, and other gear. **Hamilton Fish Park** on the Lower East Side (*128 Pitt St. at E. Houston St., tel 212/387-7691*) has an Olympic-size pool as well as a large wading pool. Also, **Riverbank State Park** (*679 Riverside Dr. at West 110th St., tel 212/694-3600, $*) has an Olympic-size pool.

nycgovparks.org and parks.ny.gov/parks/93

Upper West Side

The Upper West Side lies between Central Park and Riverside Park, and it is bounded to the south by Columbus Circle and to the north by 110th Street. Within these confines lie some of the city's most gracious residences, including ornate 19th-century brownstones that are synonymous with New York and some of the city's first luxury apartment buildings. Stroll the tree-lined streets and enjoy the rich and varied architecture, shop for everything from designer clothes to housewares at the glossy, ultramodern Time Warner Center, view cultural art at the American Folk Art Museum, and seek out world-class performances of classical music and opera at Lincoln Center. An ideal entry point into the Upper West Side for families is the American Museum of Natural History, which offers interactive displays to stimulate budding naturalists and scientists. As a tonic after savoring the sights, take in Riverside Park, less well-known than Central Park but offering just as much—with the added bonus of Hudson River views.

◖ **Tended terrace gardens brighten the front of an apartment building on the Upper West Side.**

Upper West Side

Fine architecture and two of the city's most prestigious museums come together in this well-tended corner of Manhattan.

1 American Museum of Natural History (see pp. 140–141) Take a close look at gigantic dinosaur skeletons, fascinating displays on evolution and biodiversity, and the state-of-the-art Rose Center for Earth and Space. Walk down one block.

7 Riverside Park (see p. 139)
This 330-acre (134 ha) scenic sliver, stretching from 59th Street to 158th Street along the Hudson River, has ample opportunities for recreation or quiet contemplation and incredible waterfront views of the southern end of Manhattan and New Jersey.

0 ————— 600 meters
0 ————— 600 yards

❷ New-York Historical Society
(see p. 136) Look at John James Audubon's "Birds of America" series and artifacts charting key moments in American history. Then stroll three blocks south on Central Park West.

❸ The Dakota (see pp. 136–137)
Home to many celebrities over the years, this German Renaissance-style building led the fashion for apartment living. Today it is best known as the site of John Lennon's tragic murder in 1980. Continue 12 blocks south to Columbus Circle.

❹ Deutsche Bank Center
(see p. 137) Within this complex, some of New York's best shopping and dining options await. After savoring them, head up Broadway to Lincoln Center.

❻ American Folk Art Museum (see p. 139)
One of the world's preeminent museums of folk art spans the 18th century to the present. Walk north on Broadway and turn left on West 79th Street to reach Riverside Park.

❺ Lincoln Center (see pp. 138–39)
The country's leading performing arts center includes the Metropolitan Opera House and the Juilliard School. Don't miss the chance to see and hear world-famous singers, musicians, dancers, and actors. Walk a short distance up Columbus Avenue.

UPPER WEST SIDE

UPPER WEST SIDE DISTANCE: APPROX. 4 MILES (6.4 KM)
TIME: APPROX. 7–8 HOURS SUBWAY START: 81ST ST. OR 79TH ST.

American Museum of Natural History

1 See pp. 140–141.

Central Park West at 79th St. • tel 212/769-5100 • Closed Thanksgiving and Dec. 25 • $$$$$ • Subway: B, C to 81st St.–Museum of Natural History • amnh.org

New-York Historical Society

2 Founded in 1804, the city's oldest museum, the New-York Historical Society, presents a compelling look back at the history of the United States through the lens of New York. (Even the hyphen in the museum's name, a convention used until the 1840s, is a history lesson.) The galleries display selections from 60,000 artifacts and works of art spanning four centuries, including an important **Tiffany lamp collection** and the complete **Birds of America** series, 435 watercolors by America's preeminent 19th-century wildlife artist, John James Audubon. Visitors can also peruse the research library on the second floor. Among its two million documents are dozens of standouts, including Napoleon's authorization for the **Louisiana Purchase** in 1803 and General Grant's handwritten terms of surrender to General Lee in 1865. The **Center for Women's History** profiles the lives and legacies of women who have played seminal and diverse roles in shaping the American experience.

170 Central Park West at 77th St.• tel 212/873-3400 • OClosed Mon., Thanksgiving, Dec. 25 • $$$$$ • Subway: B, C to 81st St.– Museum of Natural History • nyhistory.org

"Dragonfly Table Lamp" is one of the iconic Tiffany Studios pieces at the New-York Historical Society.

The Dakota

3 The city's most famous apartment building is notable for its ornate features as well as its roster of past and present celebrity residents. When the building, designed by Henry J. Hardenbergh, was completed in 1884, the Upper West Side was so desolate that the building was named after the remote Dakota Territory. But the distinctive, nine-story German Renaissance–style structure, with its detailed stonework, reliefs, balconies, and gables, greatly helped to transform the neighborhood. Judy Garland and Leonard Bernstein are among the Dakota's former residents, and, renamed The Bramford, it was the film home of Rosemary and John Woodhouse (Mia Farrow and John Cassavetes) in the 1968 horror classic *Rosemary's Baby*. Though designated a National Historic Landmark in 1976, it is almost impossible to step inside one of the Dakota's luxurious apartments: The residents are fiercely protective of their privacy, and a taciturn doorman guards the building's entrance at all hours.

1 West 72nd St. • Subway: B, C to 72nd St.

Deutsche Bank Center

4 The gleaming complex rising out of Columbus Circle has some of the city's best shopping, dining, entertainment, and accommodations. Formerly the Time Warner Center, it contains more than 40 shops, from the cutting edge (Montmartre and luxury skinwear purveyor Wolford) to crowd pleasers (J. Crew and Williams-Sonoma), and several high-end restaurants. Rotating art exhibits enliven the lobbies, and **Jazz at Lincoln Center** *(tel 212/258-9800, jazz.org)* runs a program of world-class live jazz concerts from several venues in the complex, including the late-night **Dizzy's Club.** Visit the stylish Mandarin Oriental hotel, on the 35th to 54th floors, for its superb views of Central Park and beyond.

10 Columbus Circle • tel 212/823-6300 • Subway: 1, A, B, C, D to 59th St.–Columbus Circle • theshopsatcolumbuscircle.com

GOOD **EATS**

■ MALECÓN
A venerable Dominican restaurant serving a huge Caribbean menu, including mofongos. **764 Amsterdam Ave., tel 212/864-5648, $$**

■ MASA
One of few NYC restaurants to be awarded three Michelin stars, the Shinto-like Masa, helmed by sushi-master chef Masayoshi Takayama, offers imaginative and sublime dishes at millionaire prices. **4th floor, The Shops at Columbus Circle, tel 212/823-9800, $$$$$**

■ PER SE
At Thomas Keller's world-famous restaurant expect the unforgettable—superb ingredients, perfect service, and a huge bill. Reservations required. **4th floor, Deutsche Bank Center, tel 212/823-9335, $$$$$**

■ WHOLE FOODS
Take your pick from a sushi bar, pizza station, and more, and nosh in the store's crowded but pleasant café. **Lower level, Deutsche Bank Center, tel 212/823-9600, $**

Lincoln Center

5 Comprising 11 arts organizations, the Lincoln Center for the Performing Arts includes the **Metropolitan Opera,** the **New York City Ballet,** and the **New York Philharmonic.** A $1.2-billion renovation, which was launched shortly before Lincoln Center's 50th anniversary in 2009, expanded and revitalized a number of buildings, including **David Geffen Hall** (formerly Alice Tully Hall), where the Chamber Society performs. Among the most spectacular venues is the **Metropolitan Opera House,** a colossal building with a gorgeous interior complete with a 24-carat gold leaf ceiling and a grand, spiraling staircase. All the world's greatest opera singers have performed here, including Luciano Pavarotti, Enrico Caruso, and Maria Callas. Though most performances command top prices, discounted day-of tickets are available at the David Rubenstein Atrium *(Broadway at 62nd St., tel 212/875-5456),* and online *(metopera.org/season/tickets/rush-page),* so it's now easier to snag coveted seats. But there are plenty of ways to enjoy Lincoln Center

A lighted fountain splashes in front of the Metropolitan Opera House at Lincoln Center.

for no money at all—the expansive plazas are great spots for strolling, and there are scores of free happenings, like the Atrium's eclectic weekly calendar of events, from its ¡VAYA! Latin music and dance series to hip-hop Shakespeare.

Between West 62nd and 65th Sts., and Columbus and Amsterdam Aves.
• tel 212/875-5456 • Subway: 1 to 66th St.–Lincoln Center • lc.lincolncenter.org

American Folk Art Museum

6 From handmade quilts and weathervanes to cookie jars and hunting decoys, this museum collects and displays folk art of the 18th and 19th centuries. While American art remains the main focus, the museum has expanded its vision to include pieces spanning nearly every continent and four centuries. Works by self-taught contemporary artists, such as Henry Darger, are another specialty, while many works among its 8,000-piece collection (from quilts to weathervanes) are displayed in special exhibitions.

2 Lincoln Square • tel 212/595-9533 • Closed Mon., Jan. 1, July 4, Thanksgiving, Dec. 25 • Subway: 1 to 66th St.–Lincoln Center • folkartmuseum.org

Riverside Park

7 Created by Frederick Law Olmsted, co-designer of Central Park, Riverside Park is much prized by local residents for its tranquility and superb facilities. Begin exploring at 70th Street, where you can also rent bicycles. **Pier 1** at 70th Street is an ideal spot for fishing and relaxing, and a summer venue for free events such as concerts and kids' shows. The park has activities for everyone, from baseball, basketball, and handball to roller hockey and skate parks. Of the park's 15 playgrounds, the **River Run Playground** (*82nd St.*), with its miniature Hudson River, is one of the best. From 83rd Street, the half-mile (0.8 km) **Serpentine Promenade,** a bike and running path, snakes past the **Soldiers' and Sailors' Memorial** to New Yorkers who died in the Civil War and the **91st Street Garden**, its lovely flowerbeds tended by die-hard volunteers.

Riverside Dr. at West 70th St. • Subway: 1, 2, 3 to 72nd St. • nycgovparks.org

American Museum of Natural History

Gain insights into life on Earth and enjoy virtual travel in space.

"The Spectrum of Life" exhibit displays thousands of specimens, from bacteria to mammals.

With its darkened galleries packed with eerily realistic dioramas and massive dinosaur skeletons, it's little wonder that kids and adults alike find this a magical place. The nearly 150-year-old institution occupies four blocks and is one of the world's most important scientific museums. Besides the memorable permanent displays, several groundbreaking exhibits are always on rotation, a Discovery Room provides kids with hands-on activities, and the renovated IMAX theater shows movies every hour.

◼ MILSTEIN FAMILY HALL OF OCEAN LIFE

A 94-foot-long (28.6 m) **model of a blue whale** hangs from the ceiling in this favorite stop-off on the first floor. High-definition video projections, interactive computer stations, and models of more than 750 sea creatures, from microscopic algae to glowing jellyfishes, all combine to immerse visitors in life under the sea.

◼ HALL OF BIODIVERSITY

Also on the first floor, this hall attracts visitors to see the psychedelic installation of specimens titled "**The Spectrum of Life.**" Even more spectacular, the interactive **rain-forest diorama** combines video, sound, and smell to simulate the experience of stepping into a rain forest. The display stresses the need to preserve the variety and interdependence of Earth's life forms.

◼ MARGARET MEAD HALL OF PACIFIC PEOPLES

This third-floor hall features the studies of the famous anthropologist Margaret Mead (1901–1978), who worked in the museum's Anthropology

Department for most of her life. The exhibition focuses on the myriad cultures of the South Pacific islands, including Polynesia and Micronesia. A group of traditional masks made of wood and bark from Papua New Guinea ranks top among its highlights.

◼ ROSE CENTER FOR EARTH AND SPACE

On ground level on the museum's north side, you will find another must-see component of the museum—the ultramodern Rose Center, a giant glass cube enveloping the Hayden Planetarium. Experience a virtual journey through space via a uniquely powerful **reality simulator,** and witness the beginnings of the universe in the **Big Bang.** Other standouts include the **Hall of Planet Earth** and the **Cosmic Pathway** that charts 13 billion years of evolution.

UPPER WEST SIDE

Central Park West at 79th St. • tel 212/769-5100 • Closed Thanksgiving and Dec. 25 • $$$$$ • Subway: B, C to 81st St.–Museum of Natural History • amnh.org

The Brownstone

No residential building in New York City is more iconic than the aptly named brownstone; long rows of these narrow, three-to-six-story homes distinguish neighborhoods on the Upper West Side and elsewhere in Manhattan and Brooklyn. They often serve as fictional residences in movies and television series—for example, the characters in Spike Lee's films habitually pass the time on the stoops of brownstones in Brooklyn.

Carved stone foliage detailing is a feature of the brownstone (above). Classic row houses fan out along Berkeley Place, Brooklyn (right).

UPPER WEST SIDE

Desirable Residences

In New York, the term "brownstone" refers to any kind of row house, whether of brick, limestone, or marble. Some of the city's first row houses started popping up in the late 18th century in lower Manhattan and were characterized by their colonial design, small size, and brick exterior. Beginning in the 1850s, brownstone, quarried in Connecticut and New Jersey, became the building material of choice. Everyone from middle-class families to the city's elite aspired to live in a brownstone, including the railroad magnate William H. Vanderbilt, who owned a $2 million pair at 640 and 642 Fifth Avenue.

Features that were subsequently added are now considered quintessential characteristics, such as a steeply sloped stoop and decorative molding around the windows and doors. By the late 1870s, much of the city was filled with densely packed brownstones, but the Upper West Side remained largely undeveloped. The introduction of an elevated train to the neighborhood in 1879 kicked off a period of huge growth. The architectural styles of this era, including Queen Anne, Romanesque, and Renaissance Revival, encouraged unusual artistic freedom and eclecticism. On the Upper West Side, the houses were visually distinct from one another, often with different colored bricks and stone on a single façade—much to the taste of their socially competitive residents.

Return to Glory

Since the 1960s, many of these buildings have been restored to their original grandeur. The Upper West Side, Chelsea, Greenwich Village, and parts of Brooklyn (see pp. 162–163) are now being celebrated for their streets of majestic row houses.

DON'T **MISS**

73rd Street, between Central Park West and Columbus Avenue—Queen Anne–style brownstones

East side of West End Avenue, between West 76th and West 77th Streets—an entire block of 1880s–1890s row houses

St. Luke's Place, between Seventh Avenue and Hudson Street—stunning 1850s Italianate row houses

Willow Street, between Pineapple and Clark Streets, Brooklyn—rare brownstone-front Gothic Revival row houses, at Nos. 118, 120, and 122

UPPER WEST SIDE

Gourmet Shops

On the Upper West Side and beyond, you don't have to go far to discover a gourmet food shop. Whether it's an old-school mom-and-pop establishment selling classic Italian imports or a new mega-store with several specialty stores under one roof, there's plenty to entice foodies to the Big Apple.

■ CITARELLA

Citarella began as a simple seafood market in Harlem in 1912. Owner Mike Citarella moved the flagship store to the Upper West Side, but his focus on quality fish didn't change. Today three stores across the city have pristine seafood counters loaded with everything from New Zealand cockles to wild bass, plus a variety of delicious prepared dishes, an excellent meat counter, and hundreds of cheeses.

2135 Broadway at 75th St. • tel 212/874-0383 • citarella.com

■ ZABAR'S

Zabar's, on the Upper West Side, is a beloved, family-owned delicatessen dating back to 1934. This is the place for smoked salmon and seafood salads, dozens of types of coffee, and delectable baked goods, like hearty rye bread and chocolate rugelach. The store's adjoining café—usually packed with elderly locals—is great for a bowl of matzo ball soup and a dense, onion knish.

2245 Broadway, between 80th and 81st Sts. • tel 212/787-2000 • zabars.com

■ EATALY

In Midtown South, Eataly is a one-stop-shop for all things Italian. Founded by Italian restaurateur and business guru Oscar Farinetti, the two-story culinary emporium includes several sit-down restaurants, casual food counters specializing in everything from paninis to gelato, and a wealth of imported Italian treats.

200 Fifth Avenue • tel 212/229-2560 • eataly.com

■ DI PALO'S FINE FOODS

Every day in Little Italy, the owners of Di Palo's Fine Foods roll up their sleeves to make a batch of fresh mozzarella and ricotta following the same family recipe used since the store first opened in 1925.

UPPER WEST SIDE

Russ & Daughters has been selling top-quality smoked fish and caviar since 1914.

Di Palo's also sells imported Italian goods, such as prosciutto, speck, and wine from all over the country.

200 Grand St. between Mulberry and Mott Sts. • tel 212/226-1033

■ DESPAÑA

This sleek SoHo shop is the city's source for everything Spanish, from hand-sliced Ibérico ham and chorizo to paella pans and earthenware dishes called *cazuelas*. A café within the store serves excellent coffee, sandwiches, and typical tapas.

408 Broome St. at Cleveland Pl. • tel 212/219-5050 • despananyc.com

■ RUSS & DAUGHTERS

At the turn of the 20th century, when the Lower East Side was home to nearly two million Eastern European Jewish immigrants, appetizing stores—shops that, in accordance with kosher dietry laws, sold fish and dairy products but no meat—were commonplace. Today, Russ & Daughters is a rare survivor. It is one of the best places for cream cheese or lox bagels and fresh orange juice. For more to nosh on, check out their café a few blocks south (*127 Orchard St.*).

179 East Houston St., bet. Allen and Orchard Sts. • tel 212/475-4880 • russanddaughters.com

The Heights & Harlem

Harlem runs the width of Manhattan from 96th Street on the south to 170th Street on the north. Until the 1970s and '80s, it was largely seen as a place to avoid, but restored brownstones, new galleries, and still thriving music venues have since made it a key part of the New York experience. African Americans flocked to the area in the early 20th century, when writers, intellectuals, and artists produced the phenomenon known as the Harlem Renaissance. El Barrio, in the southeast section, is home to a large Latino community, celebrated at the El Museo del Barrio. Washington Heights, named for George Washington, who fought there during the Revolutionary War, offers a little piece of medieval Europe in America—The Met Cloisters, an outpost of the Metropolitan Museum of Art.

○ The mural shows self-portraits by local young artists and is one of several such artworks enlivening Harlem's streets.

The Heights & Harlem

Multicultural arts and heritage beckon in Manhattan's northernmost neighborhoods.

7 Morris-Jumel Mansion (see p. 153) Peruse Manhattan's oldest house, along with views of the river. Head northwest to the 163rd St.–Amsterdam Avenue station. Take the C train to 168th Street and the A train to 190th Street. Walk through Fort Tryon Park to The Met Cloisters.

8 The Met Cloisters (see pp. 154–155) Contemplate the medieval art and architecture in this peaceful conclusion to the tour.

INWOOD HILL PARK
BROADWAY
W. 204TH ST.
DYCKMAN ST.
TENTH AVENUE
HIGH BRIDGE PARK
WASHINGTON HEIGHTS
Harlem River
HARLEM
RIVER DRIVE
HIGH BRIDGE PARK
BROADWAY
HENRY
HUDSON PARKWAY
The Met Cloisters
Morris-Jumel Mansion
WEST 155TH STREET

❶ El Museo del Barrio (see
p. 150) Begin by visiting New
York's leading Latino cultural
center. Go north up Fifth
Avenue, then turn left along
110th Street and right on
Amsterdam Avenue.

❷ The Cathedral Church
of St. John the Divine
(see p. 151) The ethos of this
great cathedral reflects local
diversity and inclusiveness.
Head west to Riverside Park.

❸ General Grant National
Memorial (see p. 151) The 18th
president and the Union's most
celebrated general of the Civil
War, Grant is entombed at this
mausoleum in Riverside Park.
Zigzag east to West 125th Street.

❹ Apollo Theater (see
p. 152) This venue has launched
the careers of many superstars.
Continue west along West
125th Street.

❺ The Studio Museum in Harlem (see
p. 152) The first U.S. museum dedicated
to black artists features African-American
art from the 19th and 20th centuries.
Head north to Adam C. Powell Boulevard,
and turn right on 138th Street.

❻ The Abyssinian Baptist
Church (see p. 153) Harlem's most
prominent church has a famed
gospel choir. From Adam C. Powell
Boulevard, take the M2 bus north
to West 160th Street and walk
west to Jumel Terrace.

THE HEIGHTS & HARLEM   DISTANCE: APPROX. 8 MILES (13 KM)
TIME: 8 HOURS   SUBWAY START: 103RD ST.

Map labels

Hudson River
Harlem River
Harlem River Drive
HARLEM
RIVERSIDE PARK
HENRY HUDSON PARKWAY
RIVERSIDE PARK
ST. NICHOLAS PARK
MORNINGSIDE PARK
MARCUS GARVEY PARK
CENTRAL PARK
CENTRAL PARK NORTH
CENTRAL PARK WEST
CATHEDRAL PARKWAY
WEST 145th STREET
SAINT NICHOLAS AVENUE
AMSTERDAM AVENUE
BROADWAY
8TH AVE
LENOX AVE
EAST 125TH STREET
EAST 116TH STREET
AVENUE
FIRST AVENUE
THIRD AVENUE
F.D.R. DRIVE

145th Street
145th St.
135th Street
125th Street
116th Street
103rd Street
110th Street–Cathedral Parkway

The Abyssinian Baptist Church
The Studio Museum in Harlem
Apollo Theater
The Cathedral Church of St. John the Divine
El Museo del Barrio
General Grant National Memorial

0 — 1 mile
0 — 1 kilometer

El Museo del Barrio

1 This museum in East (Spanish) Harlem, or El Barrio, at the top end of Fifth Avenue's Museum Mile, started life modestly in 1969 as a place to curate and display the art and history of New York's Puerto Rican community. Today, the museum's collection of more than 8,000 paintings, sculptures, photographs, and other works of art spans at least 800 years of Latino, Latin American, and Caribbean culture, from pre-Columbian Taíno artifacts to late 20th-century pieces. Highlights of the museum include "The All-Powerful Hand of Christ (La Mano Poderosa)" by Puerto Rican artist Norberto Cedeño, and a stone **Taíno ceremonial belt** (1200–1500). Signage on the exhibits is in both English and Spanish.

1230 Fifth Ave. at 104th St. • tel 212/831-7272 • $$ • Closed Mon.-Wed., Jan. 1, July 4, Thanksgiving, Dec. 25 • Subway: 6 to 103rd St. or 2, 3 to 110th St. • elmuseo.org

"La Cama" by Puerto Rican artist Pepón Osorio forms part of El Museo del Barrio's collection.

The Cathedral Church of St. John the Divine

2 One of the world's largest cathedrals has a floor area of 121,000 square feet (11,240 sq m) and a 232-foot-high (71 m) vault. Built in fits and starts beginning in 1892, in a mixture of Gothic, Romanesque, and Byzantine styles, it is still only two-thirds complete. One incomplete arch, known as **Pearl Harbor Arch,** has been left in memory of a stonecarver who never returned from World War II. The cathedral's seven **Chapels of the Tongues,** each one dedicated to a different immigrant group, reflect New York City's diversity. All are welcome here, including four-legged creatures—the annual Blessing of the Animals in October has included a tortoise, a macaw, and a yak. The grounds have a children's sculpture garden, ecology trail, and Peace Fountain. On Mondays and Fridays at 2 p.m. and on Saturdays at noon and 2 p.m., you can climb 124 feet (38 m) up spiral staircases to the top of the cathedral to study the architecture and stained-glass windows.

1047 Amsterdam Ave. at West 112th St. • tel 212/316-7540 • $ (donation) • Subway: 1, C to Cathedral Parkway • stjohndivine.org

General Grant National Memorial

3 A grand, granite mausoleum overlooking the Hudson River in the north of Riverside Park (see p. 139) is the final resting place of President Ulysses S. Grant and his wife, Julia. The tomb—the largest in North America—was completed in 1897 and is engraved with the words "Let us have peace," a line from Grant's speech to the 1868 Republican Convention that became his slogan in the subsequent presidential campaign. When the former Civil War general died in 1885, around 90,000 people donated more than $600,000 to build his tomb—then the largest public fundraising effort in U.S. history. Until World War II, it was a more popular attraction than the Statue of Liberty. During the summer, there are outdoor concerts and a ranger-led walk through Riverside Park.

Riverside Dr. at West 122nd St. • tel 646/670-7251 • Closed Mon., Tues., Jan. 1, Thanksgiving, Dec. 25 • Subway: 1 to 125th St. • nps.gov/gegr

**"Amateur Night" at the Apollo
teams up would-be stars with
vociferous audiences who revel
in the party-like atmosphere.**

Apollo Theater

④ This legendary theater, built in 1914,
launched the careers of many great
performers—including Jimi Hendrix, Gladys
Knight, the Jackson Five, and Diana Ross.
Most emerging stars got their break by winning
"Amateur Night," Ella Fitzgerald being the first
to do so in 1934. Since then audiences have
been cheering and jeering performers every
Wednesday night beginning at 7:30 p.m. You too
can join in encouraging (or not) new talent as
a succession of singers, dancers, guitarists, and
other artists bravely takes the stage. The Apollo
also hosts top acts, such as Stevie Wonder and
Salif Keita, in addition to fresh talent.

253 West 125th St. between Seventh and Eighth Aves.
• tel 212/531-5300 • Amateur Night: $$$$$ • Subway: 2, 3, A,
B, C, D to 125th St. • apollotheater.org

The Studio Museum in Harlem

⑤ Founded in 1968, the first U.S. art museum dedicated to black
artists houses 19th- and 20th-century African-American
paintings and sculptures, as well as work by artists from elsewhere
in the African diaspora. The permanent collection includes
photographs by Dawoud Bey and paintings by Jacob Lawrence and
Alma Thomas, but the crown jewels are the photographs by James
Van Der Zee. From the early 1900s until his death in 1983, Van
Der Zee chronicled the lives of the people of Harlem. The museum
temporarily closed in 2022 and is scheduled to reopen in 2024 in
a new 82,000-square-foot contemporary building that will nearly
double the exhibition space.

144 West 125th St. between Seventh Ave. and Malcolm X Blvd. • tel 212/864-4500
• $$ • Closed: Mon., Tues., Wed., and major public holidays • Subway: 2, 3, A, B, C, D to
125th St. • studiomuseum.org

The Abyssinian Baptist Church

6 New York's first African-American Baptist church offers the chance to listen to one of the nation's finest gospel choirs. Founded in 1808 by a group of African Americans and Ethiopian sea merchants, Harlem's most prominent church has more than 4,000 parishioners. If you wish to attend the 11 a.m. Sunday service, get there early; parishioners get first dibs on the church's 1,000-odd seats, and the visitors' line typically stretches around the block. Be sure to dress appropriately—no tank tops, shorts, or flip-flops; and remember that you are asked to stay for the full two-and-a-half-hour service.

132 W. 138th St. • tel 212/862-7474 • Subway: 2, 3, A, B, C to 135th St. • abyssinian.org

Morris-Jumel Mansion

7 Built in 1765, this Georgian-style mansion served as home and battle headquarters to George Washington in 1776. Located on a hilltop overlooking the Hudson River, it gave Washington a strategic advantage in the Battle of Harlem Heights against the British. Inside the house, which is Manhattan's oldest personal residence, each room is decorated to re-create a part of its history, including the colonial period, the Revolutionary War, and the new republic.

65 Jumel Ter. • tel 212/923-8008 • $$ • Closed Mon.–Wed., Jan. 1, Thanksgiving, Dec. 25, and major public holidays • $ • Subway: C to 163rd St. • morrisjumel.org

The Met Cloisters

8 See pp. 154–155.

99 Margaret Corbin Dr. • tel 212/923-3700 • Closed Wed., Jan. 1, Thanksgiving, Dec. 25 • $$$$$ • Subway: A to 190th St. • metmuseum.org/cloisters

GOOD **EATS**

■ **FAMOUS FISH MARKET**
A favored mecca for fish fry lovers, this takeout eatery has been run by the same family for half a century. Try the classic fish n' chips, a bowl of shimps and clams, or whiting served in a small paper basket or in a sliced-bread sandwich, with heapings of tartar. **684 St. Nichola Ave., 212/491-8323, $$**

■ **RED ROOSTER**
Cookbook writer and chef Marcus Samuelsson serves Southern comfort food, including blackened catfish and black-eyed peas. **310 Lenox Ave., tel 212/792-9001, $$$**

■ **SYLVIA'S RESTAURANT**
Head to this legendary spot for Sunday brunch, where you can listen to gospel music while feasting on soul food. Since opening in 1962, it's become a hot spot for residents and tourists alike. **328 Malcolm X Blvd. at West 127th St., tel 212/996-0660, $$**

The Met Cloisters

*Wander among some of the world's greatest medieval artworks
in a tranquil setting reminiscent of early monastic life.*

The columns of Saint-Guilhem-le-Désert (circa 1206) display a wealth of carved detail.

The remains of five French cloisters and other religious sites were shipped from Europe in the early 20th century by an American collector and bought by the Metropolitan Museum of Art in 1925, and added to subsequently. The Met Cloisters' collection of medieval European art and architecture—around 3,000 pieces from the ninth to the 16th centuries—is arranged in chronological order. Set above the Hudson River in Upper Manhattan's Fort Tryon Park, the whole site is invitingly small, and its displays can be viewed in a single visit.

■ Early Medieval Masterpieces

Downstairs in the Treasury, the **"Cloisters Cross"** is an intricate Romanesque altar cross made of walrus tusk, with immense visual and spiritual appeal. Although less than two feet (0.6 m) high, it is meticulously carved with 92 tiny figures and 98 inscriptions on the front and back. It is sometimes called the Bury St. Edmunds Cross, for the monastery in England where it may have originated.

Among the architectural stars are early **13th-century columns and pilasters** that are part of the Saint-Guilhem Cloister—originally from the Benedictine Abbey of Saint-Guilhem-le-Désert near Montpellier, France. The decoration includes acanthus leaf and blossom designs, while some of the capitals have a lacy effect created by skillful drilling.

■ Textiles & Fine Art

The stunning **"Unicorn Tapestries,"** in an eponymous room, depict the dramatic hunt and capture of a unicorn. These seven fantastical 15th-century wall hangings were probably commissioned by Anne of Brittany, the richest woman in Europe, to celebrate her marriage to King Louis XII of France. Beautifully preserved, the tapestries still glisten with strands of gold and silver.

In the Campin Room, a jewel-toned triptych known as the **"Merode Altarpiece"** (ca 1425), attributed to Robert Campin, depicts the Annunciation. It also shows Joseph busy in his workshop, having just made two mousetraps, and details of everyday life in a Flemish town.

■ The Gardens

The Met Cloisters' **enclosed gardens** are designed and maintained to emulate a medieval original in layout and horticulture, based on evidence from primary sources. As well as being educational, they are a great place to relax and spend a sunny day.

SAVVY TRAVELER

Hour-long tours of the collection highlights take place every afternoon. Also, from May through October daily, experts in horticulture and tree husbandry conduct lunchtime tours of the gardens. Neither tour requires extra fees or reservations.

99 Margaret Corbin Dr. • tel 212/923-3700 • Closed Wed., Jan. 1, Thanksgiving, Dec. 25 • $$$$$ • Subway: A to 190th St. • metmuseum.org/cloisters

Harlem Renaissance

Starting at the turn of the century, African Americans from across the country, especially the South, started moving north to seek better lives. They settled in Harlem beginning around 1910, and over time many made their voices heard as poets, intellectuals, and musicians in what became known as the Harlem Renaissance. All took pride in their culture and believed they were forging a greater respect for their race.

The song "I'm Just Wild about Harry" (above) from the musical *Shuffle Along* became a huge hit. The Cotton Club's brilliant musicians attracted celebrity guests (right).

Cultural Blossoming

The migration of African Americans to northern cities—especially to Harlem—in the early 20th century created a vibrant atmosphere in which black writers began to articulate the experiences of black Americans.

One of the most successful authors of the period was Langston Hughes. With poems such as "The Negro Speaks of Rivers," he wrote about what it was like to be black in America and encouraged others to do the same. Zora Neale Hurston was the leading black female writer of the period, best known for *Their Eyes Were Watching God,* one of the first novels based on a black woman's voyage of self discovery. Both writers celebrated their blackness, rejecting the role of a second-class citizen.

In 1925, African-American professor Alain Locke edited a collection of poems and essays by black writers called *The New Negro.* The book shattered stereotypes, and it was key to defining the Harlem Renaissance. Locke wrote: "In the very process of being transplanted, the Negro is

THE HEIGHTS & HARLEM

becoming transformed…. In Harlem, Negro life is seizing upon its first chances for group expression and self-determination."

All That Jazz

Southern blacks brought new rhythms with them when they moved north. Jazz musicians and singers including Louis Armstrong, Bessie Smith, and Duke Ellington performed at clubs and theaters, some of which, such as the Cotton Club and the Roseland Ballroom, only served white patrons.

Black theater also had a renaissance. *Shuffle Along* became the first all African-American musical to play on Broadway—to a white audience—in 1921. The play had a sophisticated love story and led to more firsts for African Americans in the medium.

HARLEM **JAZZ**

Harlem honors its jazz culture with clubs and a museum:

American Legion Post 398 (see p. 69)

The Cotton Club The house band still performs great jazz music in an old-style location. **656 West 125th St. at Riverside Dr., tel 212/663-7980, cottonclub-newyork.com**

Minton's (see p. 69)

The National Jazz Museum in Harlem Peruse a rich library on local jazz history. **58 West 129th St., tel 212/348-8300, jazzmuseuminharlem.org**

THE HEIG·ITS & HARLEM

BROOKLYN

Brooklyn

Artists from Walt Whitman to Spike Lee have drawn inspiration from dynamic Brooklyn. Settled by the Dutch in 1636 and named Breuckelen, it was an independent city until 1898, when it was incorporated as a borough of New York. In the ensuing years, everyone from New England farmers to European immigrants put down roots in this rural swath of land, now occupying around 71 square miles (184 sq km). Brooklyn still attracts immigrants from all over the world, making it one of the most diverse places in the United States and a great place to explore the cuisines and traditions of other cultures. What's more, Brooklyn no longer plays second fiddle to Manhattan. Over the past few decades, artists, students, families, and Manhattan defectors have sought out this now ultracool—and increasingly expensive—borough. Once-industrial areas are now buzzing hipster enclaves. Elegant Brooklyn Heights and the world-class Brooklyn Museum, along with gorgeous gardens and arts centers, quirky boutiques and top musical venues, lie just a walk away across the East River.

◀ **Gracious brownstones typify the quiet streets of Brooklyn Heights.**

BROOKLYN

❶ Brooklyn Bridge (see p. 162) **Begin** by crossing the country's most influential bridge, which inspired both architect Frank Lloyd Wright and artist Georgia O'Keeffe. Leave the bridge via Cadman Plaza West/Old Fulton Street. Walk down Middagh Street to Willow Street.

❷ Brooklyn Heights' Historic Houses (see pp. 162–163) Charming Willow Street has some of the city's best-preserved architecture. After exploring, follow Middagh Street to Columbia Heights.

❸ Brooklyn Heights Promenade (see pp. 163–164) This scenic stretch, with views across the harbor to Lower Manhattan, is ideal for strolling and photography. Take the 2 train from Clark Street to Eastern Parkway–Brooklyn Museum.

| 0 | 1000 meters |
| 0 | 1000 yards |

BROOKLYN   DISTANCE: APPROX. 7 MILES (11 KM)
TIME: 7–10 HOURS   SUBWAY START: BROOKLYN BRIDGE–CITY HALL

Brooklyn

New York's most populous borough balances tranquil green spaces and historic architecture with a thriving arts scene.

4 Brooklyn Museum (see pp. 168–169) One of the country's oldest and largest art museums houses an Egyptian collection and a center devoted to feminist art. Walk east down Eastern Parkway.

5 Brooklyn Botanic Garden (see pp. 161–165) A series of gardens-within-a-garden, this peaceful area provides delight to the horticulturist and relaxation for all. Walk northwest along Eastern Parkway to Grand Army Plaza.

6 Central Library (see p. 165) The majestic flagship of the country's fifth largest library system has rare collections and hosts regular readings, concerts, and other events. Enter Prospect Park by its main entrance in the heart of Grand Army Plaza.

7 Prospect Park (see p. 166) Lose yourself in the borough's only forest, look for rare birds, or take advantage of the park's cultural offerings. Leave the park at Plaza Street West, and then walk up Union Street to Seventh Avenue.

8 Park Slope (see pp. 166–167) For eating and shopping, you'll find yourself spoiled for choice in and around Fifth and Seventh Avenues in this sought-after neighborhood.

Brooklyn Bridge

1 One of the engineering marvels of the 19th century, the world's first steel suspension bridge, completed in 1883, overawed onlookers with its size (see p. 170). Awe-inspiring it was, but also serviceable: In 1884, circus-founder P. T. Barnum paraded over it with 21 elephants to demonstrate its safety. Today, whether you walk, run, skate, or bike over it, crossing the Brooklyn Bridge is a must for any visitor to New York City. Unparalleled views of Manhattan, the East River, and the Statue of Liberty unfold before your eyes, along with an up-close look at the bridge's massive, neo-Gothic towers and criss-crossing wire cables, inviting myriad photo opportunities. Starting in Manhattan's Financial District, a walk across the 6,000-foot-long (1,830 m) bridge takes about 45 minutes. Pedestrians use an elevated footpath separated from the traffic below.

Access the bridge at Park Row and Centre St., Manhattan • tel 718/222-9939 • Subway: 4, 5, 6 to Brooklyn Bridge–City Hall • Exit at Tillary and Adams Sts. or Prospect St., Brooklyn • nycgo.com

Brooklyn Heights' Historic Houses

2 Few New York neighborhoods rival Brooklyn Heights for its historic buildings. Some of the borough's first brick houses and brownstones (see pp. 142–143) were built here after 1814, when a regular ferry service between Manhattan and Brooklyn was established. Designated New York's first historic district in 1965, the neighborhood has since been protected from invasive development. A walk down **Willow Street** reveals some of the handsomest and most architecturally diverse buildings. Highlights include **Nos. 108, 110,** and **112,** three Queen Anne–style row houses built in 1880; and **Nos. 155, 157,** and **159,** redbrick, Federal-style homes from 1826 that have their original doorways and ironwork. Other gems await on the streets that cross Willow—Cranberry, Orange, Pineapple, and Clark Streets. Three blocks south, **Our Lady of Lebanon Maronite Cathedral** (*113 Remsen St., tel 718/624-7228, ololc.org*), completed in 1846 by architect Richard Upjohn,

Under the Brooklyn Bridge, the River Café commands spectacular views of Lower Manhattan.

who designed Wall Street's Trinity Church (see p. 47), was the first Romanesque Revival–style building constructed in America. To soak up more of the borough's history, head back two blocks to the **Center for Brooklyn History** *(128 Pierrepoint St., tel 718/222-4111, $$, closed Mon. and Tues., brooklynhistory.org)*. Carved figures decorate the terra-cotta Queen Anne building, designed by architect George B. Post in 1881. Inside, exhibits range from Brooklyn's beloved sports team, the Dodgers, to its long and illustrious history of beer brewing.

Willow St. runs between Middagh and Pierrepoint Sts. • Subway: 2, 3 to Clark St.

Brooklyn Heights Promenade

3 One of the most picturesque and romantic spots in the city, this promenade is perched high above the East River and the Brooklyn Queens Expressway (BQE), with lovely views of the harbor, Lower Manhattan, and the Brooklyn Bridge. Stretching for one-third of a mile

(0.5 km) between Remsen and Orange Streets, the parklike expanse draws everyone from tourists and old-timers, to teenage couples and families. Completed in 1950 under the influential city builder Robert Moses, the promenade was created, in part, to appease residents who opposed the construction of the BQE. The design works surprisingly well; even the noise of cars whizzing below is soothing, calling to mind rushing water more than traffic. Along the way, watch for a stone marking the land where George Washington's headquarters stood during the Revolutionary War, and a granite thunderbird honoring the Canarsie Indians who lived in the area.

Access the promenade from Middagh St.–Columbia Heights • tel 718/965-8900 • Subway: 2, 3 to Clark St. • nycgovparks.org

Brooklyn Museum

4 See pp. 168–169.

200 Eastern Parkway • tel 718/638-5000 • Closed Mon. and Tues. • $$$$ • Subway: 2,3 to Eastern Parkway–Brooklyn Museum • brooklynmuseum.org

The Brooklyn Botanic Garden combines riotous flower plantings with a calming Japanese garden.

Brooklyn Botanic Garden

5 A horticultural triumph, the 52-acre (21 ha) Brooklyn Botanic Garden has been one of the borough's great attractions since 1910. Immaculately maintained, the garden, which is home to wild rabbits, ducks, and turtles, seems instantly to induce a state of calm. Among its highlights are more than 200 cherry trees, which blossom in April. Set among rolling hills, the **Japanese Hill-and-Pond Garden** incorporates traditional elements such as a Shinto shrine by the pond, overhung with evergreen trees that make this a truly meditative spot. Other highlights include a **rose garden** with more than 1,400 varietals; an outstanding **orchid collection,**

including the giant species, *Grammatophyllum speciosum;* a **Discovery Garden** with hands-on activities for children; and a **Bonsai Museum** with 350 trees. A **Fragrance Garden** for the sight-impaired, created in 1955, is the first of its kind in the country. The area encourages visitors to smell and touch plants such as Corsican mint, Indian patchouli, and lavender. A gallery on the lower level of the **Steinhardt Conservatory** has a multimedia display about the natural world and sustainability, and installations by artists in residence.

900 Washington Ave. or 150 Eastern Parkway • tel 718/ 623-7200 • Closed Mon. and major holidays • $$$$ • Subway: B, Q to Prospect Park; 2 to Eastern Parkway–Brooklyn Museum • bbg.org

Central Library

6 The crown jewel of the 60-branch Brooklyn Public Library system, the majestic Central Library is conveniently located just steps away from the Brooklyn Botanic Garden. Constructed in 1941 in contemporary art moderne style—a variant of art deco—the building resembles an open book, with the spine on Grand Army Plaza and the library's two wings opening like book covers along Eastern Parkway and Flatbush Avenue. The grand, recently redesigned entrance and plaza form a pleasant backdrop for a free summer concert series. The branch also hosts regular author talks, book discussions, and film screenings. The library houses the **Brooklyn Collection,** composed of historic photographs, drawings, memorabilia, and the complete archive of the *Brooklyn Eagle* newspaper (1841–1963). The poet and local resident Walt Whitman served as editor of the newspaper for two years.

10 Grand Army Plaza • tel 718/230-2100 or 718/968-7275 • Subway: 2, 3 to Grand Army Plaza • brooklynpubliclibrary.org

GOOD **EATS**

■ **BROOKLYN ICE CREAM FACTORY**
Facing the East River in a historic fireboat house, this venue sells delectable ice cream in eight classic flavors. **14 Old Fulton St., tel 718/522-5211, $**

■ **GRIMALDI'S**
Just under the Brooklyn Bridge, Grimaldi's is a coal-brick-oven pizzeria. Despite the long line, you'll be seated in 30 minutes. **1 Front St., tel 718/858-4300, $$**

■ **THE RIVER CAFÉ**
On the waterfront with stunning views of Manhattan, the Michelin-starred River Café is a ravishing venue for brunch, lunch, or dinner, and it has produced some of the city's best chefs. **1 Water St., tel 718/522-5200, $$$$$**

Prospect Park

7 Central Park may be more famous, but Brooklynites are fiercely loyal to Prospect Park, a 585-acre (237 ha) sweep of woods, hills, lakes, and waterfalls. Constructed by Central Park's designers, Frederick Law Olmsted and Calvert Vaux, and opened in 1867, Prospect Park has opportunities to relax, go boating, enjoy live music, and cozy up to farm animals. The **Audubon Center** at the Boathouse *(Lincoln Road–Ocean Avenue entrance),* housed in a 1905 beaux arts building, contains an information center and kid-friendly exhibits. From here, scenic trails snake through the forest and pass by the 60-acre (24 ha) lake. Bird lovers will be delighted by the park's 200-species bird population, which includes green herons and red-tailed hawks. On Saturdays, a **farmer's market** *(Grand Army Plaza entrance)* overflows with produce. In summer, the **Lena Horne Bandshell** *(Prospect Park West and 9th Street)* hosts performances by world-famous artists, and the New York Philharmonic Orchestra offers free concerts on the **Long Meadow.** Check out the **Prospect Park Zoo** *(Lincoln Road–Ocean Avenue entrance),* where youngsters can feed the farm animals.

IN **THE KNOW**

If your visit to Brooklyn happens to coincide with a weekend, there are a couple markets worth making a detour for. **Brooklyn Flea** *(80 Pearl St. at Anchorage Place, weekends April-Dec.),* in DUMBO, for "Down Under the Brooklyn Bridge," captures Brooklyn's DIY spirit. Hipsters jostle among vendors selling jewelry, art, crafts, and more. **Smorgasburg** *(Marsha P. Johnson State Park, 90 Kent Ave; and Prospect Park's Breeze Hill (entrance at Lincoln Rd.),* **is an** all-food version of the Flea run by the same people. Here, 100 Brooklyn vendors offer bites ranging from Asian-inspired tacos to artisanal popsicles.

95 Prospect Park West • tel 718/965-8951 • Audubon Center: tel 718/287-3400 • Closed Mon.–Fri. Feb.–March; Mon.–Wed. April–Sept. except public holidays; and Oct.–Jan. • Subway: 2, 3 to Grand Army Plaza or Q to Prospect Park or F, G to 15th St.–Prospect Park • prospectpark.org

Park Slope

8 Park Slope is well-known for its stunning brownstones, popular music venues, and family-friendly eateries and stores. Head northwest along Union Street and take a left on

Statue of James Samuel Thomas Stranahan, father of Prospect Park

Seventh Avenue, to explore one of the area's charming, café-lined thoroughfares. Try **Runner Up** *(367 7th Ave., $$$)* outdoor wine bar, serving health-conscious snacks; retro-inspired **Norm's Pizza** *(388 7th Ave., $$)* for classic NY chewy-crust pizza; and **LORE** *(441 7th Ave., $$$),* offering Indian-inspired dishes such as sea bream served with a mint yogurt sauce. Or explore some of the quiet, scenic side streets in the area. Those on the right lead toward **Fifth Avenue,** which is packed with new boutiques and restaurants. **al di la Trattoria** *(248 5th Ave., tel 718/783-4565, $$$),* an elegant Italian spot, was one of the first restaurants to put Brooklyn on the culinary map. If you're looking for late-night entertainment, check out **Union Hall** *(702 Union St., tel 718/638-4400).* This is a converted warehouse complete with outdoor garden seating and a stage that regularly features comedians and musicians.

Between Union St. and Prospect Expressway, and 4th Ave. and Prospect Park
• Subway: R to Union St. or F, G, R to 4th Ave.–9th St. • nycgo.com

Brooklyn Museum

One of the country's largest art museums has a world-class collection that ranges from Egyptian mummies to contemporary art.

For his show "Unbranded," Hank Willis Thomas made 41 photographs from media imagery.

Housed in a 560,000-square-foot (52,000 sq m) beaux arts building with a glass entrance pavilion, this venerable institution is sited right by Brooklyn Botanic Garden and has been at the heart of Brooklyn's cultural life since 1823. In addition to five floors of permanent installations embracing the world's cultures, special exhibitions showcase items from the collection that are rarely seen, as well as the work of such prominent artists as Annie Leibovitz and Takashi Murakami.

■ African Galleries

Galleries on the first floor focus on West and Central African sculpture, including a **16th-century ivory gong** made for the king of Benin and a gorgeous 36-inch-tall (92 cm) **beaded Nigerian crown** of the late 1800s.

■ Islamic Galleries

The encyclopedic Islamic displays on the second floor span a wide geographic area and range of objects. Among the most famous are several **Persian works** from the late 18th century, costumes from Turkmenistan, and the **"Battle of Karbala,"** a large Qajar-dynasty oil painting depicting the martyrdom of Husayn ibn Ali, the grandson of the prophet Muhammad.

■ Egyptian Galleries

On the third floor, seven galleries chart the evolution of Egyptian art over four millennia. Highlights include a large chlorite **head of a princess; mummies** encased in intricately painted *cartonnages* (casings); and a **Book of the Dead** scroll. One of the oldest works in the museum is a **stylized female figure** from the Predynastic Period (3500–3400 B.C.).

SAVVY **TRAVELER**

First Saturdays, held from 5 p.m. to 11 p.m. on the first Saturday of every month, is a riotously fun, free event with live music and performances, artist-led talks, hands-on art projects, and the chance to roam the museum's galleries after hours. Dine at the venue's **The Norm** *(tel 646/656-0368, $$$)* restaurant or head to **the museum's Café or BKM Food Truck** *($)* for snacks and a glass of beer.

Elizabeth A. Sackler Center for Feminist Art

The center of this unique fourth-floor exhibition of feminist art is **"The Dinner Party,"** an installation by Judy Chicago. This massive, triangular banquet has 39 place settings for important women from history, from the poet Sappho to the abolitionist and women's rights activist Sojourner Truth.

■ Luce Center for American Art

This extensive exhibition on the fifth floor displays American paintings, silver, and textiles from the colonial period to today, including iconic portraits of George Washington. **Visible Storage** displays rare works usually held in storage, such as Tiffany lamps.

200 Eastern Parkway • tel 718/638-5000 • Closed Mon. and Tues. • $$$ • Subway: 2,3 to Eastern Parkway–Brooklyn Museum • brooklynmuseum.org

Bridges

As much an enduring symbol of New York as the city's other great structures, the Brooklyn Bridge was the first-ever bridge to link Manhattan Island to a populous outer borough (which, in the case of Brooklyn, was its own city at the time). Since then other mighty bridges have swung into place, overcoming the need to navigate the choppy waters, winter fogs, and freeze-ups on the city's waterways, and forging their own stories along the way.

BROOKLYN

A shared pedestrian and bike path runs along the center of the Brooklyn Bridge (above). Queensboro Bridge at sunrise (right).

Spanning History

New York's more than 2,000 bridges (including 25 movable bridges) form a vital link in the city's infrastructure, carrying everything from cars, trucks, and subway trains to bicycles, pedestrians, and even water mains. The first to be built was the timber-decked King's Bridge in 1693, between Manhattan and the Bronx. It was demolished in 1917.

Oldest Structures

Highbridge (1848), the city's oldest bridge still standing, carries a water main across the Harlem River. The **Brooklyn Bridge** (see p. 162) is the oldest vehicle bridge. Opened in 1883, it was the world's longest span for more than 20 years—and like so many fabled structures, it's supposed to be cursed. Designer John Augustus Roebling died from injuries sustained while taking measurements for the towers. His son Washington was crippled by the bends while overseeing underwater work, but, determined to continue, he supervised the project from afar by watching through a telescope.

Breaking Records

The **Verrazzano-Narrows,** with a central span of 4,260 feet (1,230 m), links Brooklyn and Staten Island and was named for Giovanni da Verrazzano, who discovered what is now New York harbor in 1524. It was the world's longest suspension bridge when it opened in 1964. On the first Sunday of November, more than 50,000 runners shuffle across it at the start of the New York City Marathon. Verrazzano-Narrows designer Othmar H. Ammann also engineered the **George Washington Bridge** (1931), which crosses the Hudson River between Manhattan's Upper West Side and New Jersey. It's also New York's largest bridge, as well as the world's busiest, carrying more than 104 million vehicles every year.

The **Ed Koch Queensboro Bridge** connects Manhattan and Queens across the East River. Completed in 1909, the bridge quickly earned New Yorkers' affections—novelist F. Scott Fitzgerald thought it made Manhattan appear wildly beautiful.

Parks & Gardens

Central Park (see pp. 120–131) may be New York's premier green space, but it is far from the only place where you can get back to nature. The Manhattan landmark is only the fifth largest of the city's 29,000 public parks and gardens; the biggest, at 2,800 acres (1,133 ha), is the Staten Island Greenbelt.

■ Brooklyn Botanic Garden
More than 10,000 plants from around the world fill the Brooklyn Botanic Garden (see pp. 164–165). Admire English cottage-garden planting in the **Shakespeare Garden,** or luxuriate in the warmth of the lush **Tropical Pavilion.**

■ Prospect Park
Across Flatbush Avenue from the Brooklyn Botanic Garden lies Prospect Park (see p. 166), where Brooklyn's last stand of indigenous forest awaits. Summer concerts, a performing arts festival in June, and a winter ice-skating rink feature among the annual events.

■ Gateway National Recreation Area
Besides Prospect Park, Brooklyn's other large green space is Gateway National Recreation Area, which covers many of **Jamaica Bay's islands.** Its 32 square miles (83 sq km) form a wildlife refuge. Opportunities for birding, walking, swimming, kayaking, picnicking, and fishing are legion.

Jamaica Bay Wildlife Refuge • tel 718/354-4606 • Subway: A, S to Broad Channel •nps.gov/gate

■ The New York Botanical Garden
The New York Botanical Garden sprawls across 250 acres (100 ha) in the heart of the borough and is home to 50 distinct gardens and plant collections. They include the habitats housed in the **Enid A. Haupt Conservatory** and a stand of old growth New York forest (oak, birch, beech, and ash) that has never been logged.

2900 Southern Blvd. • tel 718/817-8700 • Closed Mon., Thanksgiving and Dec 25 • $$$$$ • Railroad: Metro–North Harlem line from Grand Central to Botanical Garden • nybg.org

The New York Botanical Garden's Victorian conservatory is the largest in the United States.

■ PELHAM BAY PARK

Wildlife is a theme of this park on the Bronx's eastern edge. Pelham Bay includes inland areas and 13 miles (21 km) of shoreline on Long Island Sound. The park encompasses extensive woodland, saltwater marsh, and three islands. Explore by foot, bike, or horse along numerous trails, or navigate the coast by canoe. Visit **Thomas Pell Wildlife Sanctuary** for a chance to spot raccoons, coyotes, egrets, hawks, and many other species.

Pelham Bay • tel 718/430-1891 • Subway: 6 to Pelham Bay Park; Bus Bx 29 to Rodmans Neck • nycgovparks.org/parks/pelham-bay-park

■ STATEN ISLAND GREENBELT CONSERVANCY

The city's most remote slice of parkland meanders through the middle and eastern parts of the island borough and comprises several contiguous green spaces including **High Rock** and **Willowbrook** parks, and 260-foot-high (79 m) **Moses' Mountain.** In addition to hiking and biking on six major trails, you can partake in classes and events at the **Greenbelt Nature Center** (*700 Rockland Ave., tel 718/351-3450*).

Staten Island • tel 718/667-2165 • Ferry from Whitehall Terminal, Manhattan; Bus S61 to Greenbelt Nature Center • sigreenbelt.org

PART 3

Travel Essentials

TRAVEL ESSENTIALS

PLANNING YOUR TRIP

When To Go

The best months to see New York are September and October, when summer heat has eased and parks are full of fall color. Late spring is also a good choice—expect showers March to May, but with temperatures between 48°F and 68°F (9°C to 20°C). June through September averages 58°F to 83°F (14°C to 28°C), with July and August the hottest, most humid months. At this time, however, there are many outdoor attractions, such as concerts. The city looks beautiful in winter, and there are seasonal attractions such as ice skating and Christmas markets. Temperatures plummet from December to February, averaging from 23°F to 40°F (-5°C to 4°C). Whatever the season, you will be spending time both walking outdoors and exploring indoor attractions, so dress in layers year-round.

Visitor Information

New York City's **Visitor Information Center** (tel 212/484-1200, nycgo.com) has useful information. For a personalized introduction to the city, contact **Big Apple Greeter** (tel 212/669-8198, bigapplegreeter.org). This non-profit organization will match knowledgeable New Yorkers with visitors. Reserve two–three weeks in advance.

Useful Websites

nymag.com New York magazine, for listings of restaurants and entertainment. **mta.info** Metropolitan Transit Authority, for schedules and maps of city subways and buses. **nyrestroom.com** Lists the city's public restrooms.

Notable Events & Festivals

JANUARY

Winter (Antiques) Show Park Avenue Armory, tel 917/960-6559, thewintershow.com **Restaurant Week** (all around town), nycgo.com

FEBRUARY

Chinatown Lunar New Year Parade betterchinatown.com **Fashion Week** nyfw.com

MARCH

St. Patrick's Day Parade Fifth Avenue, nycstpatricksparade.org **Macy's Flower Show** Herald Square, tel 212/494-4495, macys.com/s/flower-show

APRIL

Baseball season New York Yankees, Yankee Stadium, tel 212/726-5337, mlb.com/yankees; New York Mets, Citi Field, tel 718/507-8499, mlb.com/mets **New York International Auto Show** Jacob Javits Center, tel 718/746-5300, autoshowny.com

MAY

Bike New York, Five Borough Bike Tour tel 212/682-2340, bike.nyc **Fleet Week** West Side Piers, tel 757/322-2853, fleetweeknewyork.com **Ninth Avenue International Food Festival** from 37th to 57th Streets, tel 212/581-7029, ninthavenuefoodfestival.com **Washington Square Outdoor Art Exhibit** tel 212/982-6255, wsoae.org **Westminster Kennel Club Dog Show** Madison Square Garden, westminsterkennelclub.org

JUNE

Museum Mile Festival Fifth Avenue from 82nd to 104th Streets, tel 212/606-2296, mcny.org/museummile **NYC Pride March** Fifth Avenue between 52nd Street and Greenwich Village, tel 212/807-7433 nycpride.org **Coney Island Mermaid Parade** tel 718/372-5159, coneyisland.com **Tribeca Film Festival** tel 212/941-2400, tribecafilm.com

JULY

4th of July Dramatic fireworks display on the Hudson River macys.com/social/fireworks **Lincoln Center Summer for the City** tel 212/875-5375, lincolncenter.org **Restaurant Week** (all around town) nycgo.com

AUGUST

Lincoln Center Summer for the City tel 212/875-5375, lincolncenter.org

U.S. Open Tennis Flushing Meadows Park, Queens, tel 800-990-8782, usopen.org

SEPTEMBER
West Indian-American Day Parade Eastern Parkway, Brooklyn, tel 718/467-1797, wiadca.com
New York Film Festival Lincoln Center, tel 212/875-5600, filmlinc.org
BAM Next Wave Festival Brooklyn Academy of Music, tel 718/636-4100, bam.org
Fashion Week nyfw.com

OCTOBER
Blessing of the Animals The Cathedral Church of St. John the Divine, tel 212/316-7540, stjohndivine.org
Greenwich Village Halloween Parade Sixth Ave., Spring St.–21st St., halloween-nyc.com

NOVEMBER
New York City Marathon tel 212/423-2249, tcsnycmarathon.org
Radio City Christmas Spectacular tel 212/465-6000, radiocity.com
Macy's Thanksgiving Day Parade West 77th St. and Central Park West to 34th St. and Broadway, macys.com/parade
New York Comedy Festival, theaters all around town, nycomedyfestival.com

DECEMBER
Christmas Tree Lighting Rockefeller Center, tel 212/588-8601, rockefellercenter.com

Midtown Holiday Windows Fifth Avenue, between 42nd and 57th Streets, and Madison Avenue, between 55th and 60th Streets
New Year's Eve Times Square, tel 212/768-1560, timessquarenyc.org

GETTING FROM THE AIRPORTS

John F. Kennedy International Airport or **JFK** is in southern Queens, jfkairport.com
LaGuardia on Long Island in Queens primarily serves flights within North America, laguardiaairport.com
Newark Liberty International Airport is in Newark, New Jersey, *newarkairport.com*
Port Authority NY NJ information on transportation to and from these airports, panynj.gov

Buses
GOAirlink has regular buses between JFK, LaGuardia, and Newark airports and Grand Central Terminal, Penn Station, and the Port Authority Bus Terminal, tel 212/812-9000, goairlinkshuttle.com
SuperShuttle runs between JFK and LaGuardia and most hotels, tel 800/258-3826, supershuttle.com
Newark Airport Express runs between Newark airport and Midtown Manhattan, tel 877/894-9155, coachusa.com

Car Services
Car companies offering pickups

to and from the airport include **Carmel** *(tel 212/666-6666 or 866/666-6666, carmellimo.com);* and **Airlink,** hotel pickup for up to 11 passengers *tel 212/812-9000, goairlinkshuttle.com).* **Taxis** to and from JFK: flat rate of $70 to and from Manhattan, excluding tolls and tip; taxis to and from LaGuardia: by the meter, around $24–$44, excluding tolls and tip; taxis from Newark: by the meter $50–$70, excluding tolls and tip. Book 24 hours in advance.

GETTING AROUND TOWN

As with many other great cities, there's no better way to experience New York than by using your own two feet. A car in Manhattan is more of a hindrance than a help, as traffic is always heavy and on-street parking hard to find. If you do drive into town, park your car at your hotel or a public garage ($20–$50 or more per day) and use the city's taxis, subways, and buses—these are by far the most convenient ways to get around the city.

Orienting Yourself
For the most part, the city's basic street grid makes it easy to navigate. In Manhattan, numbered streets run east-west from First Street down in the East Village to 220th Street at the northern tip. Avenues run north-south and are numbered

from First to Twelfth, increasing as you move west. However, Lexington, Madison, and Park Avenues fall between Third and Fifth Avenues, superseding Fourth Avenue. And, although maps and street signs refer to "The Avenue of the Americas," most New Yorkers still call it by its former name, Sixth Avenue.

Broadway meanders along the route of an old Indian trail and has little relation to the grid. And in much of Lower Manhattan, you'd do well to bring a compass: Streets angle off every which way, as they were laid out before the city planners took over.

Manhattan is divided into the East and West Sides, with Fifth Avenue the central axis.

If you're looking for a specific address, remember that building numbers advance out from Fifth Avenue on either side. So make sure you're clear what you're looking for: 300 *East* 23rd Street, for example, is very different from 300 *West* 23rd Street. Pay attention to the numbers of cross streets that often form part of an address to make it easier to find, such as 945 Madison Avenue at 75th Street.

Buses & Subways

Covering most of the city, buses and subway trains, at press time, cost $2.75 a ride with a MetroCard (see below)—half price for seniors and disabled, free for children under 3 feet 8 inches (1.1 m), including a transfer. Subways are ideal for long distances and during rush hour. Buses can be

scenic and relaxing but slow.
Lost and Found for buses and subways, tel 877/690-5116.
MetroCards are available at all subway stations and at many newsstands. Fare is deducted each time you enter the subway or ride a bus; the card allows for a free transfer from the subway to or from a connecting bus within a two-hour period. Subways and buses require MetroCards, or payment by contactless OMKY card-reader (cash is no longer accepted).
Key Subway Routes
1: The 1 train takes you to sites on Broadway between 42nd Street and Manhattan's northern tip (including Times Square, Lincoln Center, Columbus Circle–Central Park, and the Cathedral Church of St. John the Divine).
N & R: These two trains are good for sites on Broadway from 42nd Street south to City Hall (including Times Square, Union Square, the Villages, and SoHo). They continue on to Wall Street and the island's historic southern tip.
C: The C is good for sites on the West Side between West 4th and 168th Streets (such as the High Line, Columbus Circle–Central Park, and the American Museum of Natural History). The legendary A express train travels the same route, but skips some stops that the C always makes.
6: This is your best option for sites on the East Side, from City Hall to 125th Street (including the East Village, Grand Central, The Met, and

the Guggenheim). The 4 and 5 also run express along this line.
L: The L runs east-west along 14th Street between First and Eighth Avenues.
S: This train runs east-west on 42nd Street from Grand Central Terminal to Times Square.

Mass Transit Information: tel 877/690-5116, mta.info

Public Transportation Tips
■ Some trains and buses are local, some express. Know where you're getting off to avoid overshooting your mark or waiting through many local stops unnecessarily.
■ Between Houston and 42nd Streets, any subway you catch (except the L and S; see Key Subway Routes) will be going north-south. To get across town in that area, a bus is your only public transportation option.
■ Buses only stop when someone wants to get on or off: Push the yellow strip along the wall to alert the bus driver your stop is coming up.
■ You'll find free subway maps at all stations and bus maps on the buses. Complete information is available at mta.info.

Taxis
Take only yellow (Manhattan) or green (outer borough) cabs with medallion numbers on the roof and rates on the door. They are available if the medallion number is lit. The base fare is $3.00, then 70 cents for every additional fifth

of a mile (four blocks) or every minute in stopped or slow traffic. There's also a $2.50 peak-hour surcharge and a $1 night surcharge, plus other surcharges. There is no charge for other passengers or luggage. Tips are expected to be 15 percent.
NY Water Taxi runs ferries around Manhattan's perimeter and to Brooklyn, tel 212/742-1969, nywatertaxi.com

Hailing Taxis

To flag down one of New York's 13,000-plus licensed yellow cabs, station yourself along any busy avenue or street and start scanning for a rooftop light with its number illuminated. If it's out, the cab's taken. If the "off duty" lights are lit, the cabbie is going home. A raised arm is usually enough to get a cab, though you may be competing with other people. If somebody's got an arm up for an oncoming cab, don't try to steal it; the unwritten rule is first come, first served. Once inside, you'll find that your cabbie's expertise regarding side streets and traffic patterns is top-notch.

PRACTICAL ADVICE

The New York of today is a far cry from the New York of the 1970s, when crime was rampant and whole sections of the city were no-go zones. Now New York consistently ranks among the country's

safest large cities. That said, do keep a few things in mind:
■ Don't give your bags to anyone in an airport or train/bus station other than authorized personnel.
■ Only take official yellow taxis from the airport. Their rates are set by the city, unlike those of Uber and unlicensed operators.
■ Carry your wallet in a place you can be constantly mindful of (not a back pocket), and be sure all bags are always securely closed and in your possession, even in restaurants and stores.
■ Don't feel guilty or intimidated into giving money to performers and panhandlers you encounter on the streets and subways; you can say, "Sorry, no."
■ Have a clear idea of where you're going when visiting the outer boroughs. The streets aren't laid out as logically as in Manhattan, most are named rather than numbered, it can be challenging to hail a taxi, and subways aren't as easy to find. At night, some areas can get uncomfortably desolate.
■ While city parks aren't necessarily dangerous at night, you'll want to tune your awareness up an extra notch. Use common sense when it comes to particularly dark or empty sections.
■ When using the subways at night, make a point of riding the center cars, which are usually more crowded.
■ Be aware of those around you when using ATMs, and don't count your money on the street.

TRAVELERS WITH DISABILITIES

Airport Travelers' Aid tel 718/656-4870.
Asser Levy Playground has a playground for disabled children and a free outdoor pool, East 23rd St. at Asser Levy Place, near the East River, tel 212/447-2020, nycgovparks.org/parks/asserlevy
Big Apple Greeter offers information for disabled travelers and tours led by volunteers, tel 212/669-6216, bigapplegreeter.org
Commission for the Blind and Visually Handicapped has an office in Harlem, 163 W. 125 St., Suite 1315, tel 212/961-4440
Lighthouse International offers resources and assistance to visually impaired travelers, 250 West 64th St., tel 800-284-4422, lighthouse.org
Metropolitan Transport Authority provides useful information on accessible travel, including paratransit service, tel 877/337-2017, mta.info/accessibility

EMERGENCIES

In an emergency, call 911.
■ Crime Victims Hotline, tel 212/577-7777
■ Poison Control Center, tel 800/222-1222
■ Medical emergencies: Proceed to the nearest emergency room (call 311 for the nearest hospital) or call 911 for an ambulance.

HOTELS

The selection and price range of places to stay in New York is remarkably varied, with options to meet every taste and budget. There are as many bargains available as in any other place, with low-cost options that include bed-and-breakfasts and small older hotels in some of the most interesting neighborhoods. Check out which part of the city you'll be spending most of your vacation in, and find a hotel to match your budget. You may wish to spend a few days in an inexpensive place and then splurge on one night in one of the city's most luxurious hotels. Also try to reserve in advance, as some of the best rooms can fill up early.

Once you determine your total room budget, decide what neighborhood or area appeals to you and then research in depth. From Lower Manhattan to the Upper East and West Sides and beyond, the city teems with shopping, sight-seeing, and cultural and historic attractions. If you are drawn more to Broadway or other West Side attractions, then a place in the Times Square or Lincoln Center area may be best.

Be sure to calculate transportation into both your time and money budgets. Taxis are usually available, but a ride from the West Village to the Upper East Side, for example, can be quite expensive and also—depending on traffic—slow. If you have limited time in the city, choosing a hotel by location is imperative, to avoid spending half your trip in subways or stuck in traffic.

For disabled access, it is recommended you check with the hotel to establish the extent of its facilities. Also verify parking or access to parking spaces. Most New York hotels are air-conditioned.

Organization
Hotels listed here have been grouped first according to neighborhood, then listed alphabetically by price range.

Credit Card Abbreviations:
AE (American Express); MC (Mastercard); V (Visa).

Price Range

HOTELS
An indication of the cost of a double room in the high season is given by **$** signs.

$$$$$	Over $450
$$$$	$350–$450
$$$	$250–$350
$$	$150–$250
$	Under $150

Text Symbols
- **ⓘ** *No. of Guest Rooms*
- **🚇** *Subway*
- **🏊** *Outdoor Pool*
- **🏋** *Health Club*
- **💳** *Credit Cards Accepted*

LOWER MANHATTAN

■ Hotel on Rivington
$$$$$
107 RIVINGTON STREET
(BETWEEN LUDLOW AND ESSEX STREETS)
TEL 212/475-2600
hotelonrivington.com
This 21-story glass tower in the historic Lower East Side offers terrific city views from the floor-to-ceiling glass windows in every room. Cutting-edge designers injected creativity into all aspects of the hotel's concept and chic look. Many of the rooms have balconies, and unusual amenities include Japanese soaking tubs and in-room spa services.
ⓘ *94 rooms, 16 suites* 🚇 *F to Delancey, J to Essex St.*
💳 *All major cards*

■ Millenium Downtown
$$$$$
55 CHURCH STREET
TEL 212/693-2001
millenniumhotels.com
This top-end Financial District destination, alongside the World Trade Center site, gleams with high-tech style. There is a plasma TV and high-speed internet access in each room,

a gym, pool, cocktail bar, Church & Dey restaurant, and some beautiful views of New York Harbor. Lower rates are available on weekends.

🛈 561 🚇 1 to Cortlandt St.; C to World Trade Center 🚇 🍴 🅿️ All major cards

■ SoHo Grand
$$$$$
310 W. BROADWAY (BETWEEN GRAND & CANAL STREETS)
TEL 212/965-3000
sohogrand.com
A striking chic retro design and a fashionable, pet-friendly destination greets those who enjoy the downtown vantage point. Endless interesting stores and galleries are within walking distance.

🛈 367 + 4 suites 🚇 A, C, E to Canal St. 🍴 🅿️ All major cards

■ Gild Hall
$$$
15 GOLD STREET (AT PLATT STREET)
TEL 212/232-7700
thompsonhotels.com
Fresh from a mid-century-inspired redesign, the Gild Hall is a departure from the more traditional hotels clustered around the Financial District. Among its attractions are a library bar spread over two levels, an elegant cocktail and wine bar, and sumptuous leather bench seats in the Felice Ristorante serving Tuscan fare.

🛈 126 🚇 2, 3 to Fulton St. 🅿️ All major cards

THE VILLAGES

■ The Standard, East Village

$$$$$
25 COOPER SQUARE (BOWERY AND FIFTH STREET)
TEL 212/475-5700
standardhotels.com/east-village
A chic hotel whose curved, glassy, 21-story tower was built around an 1845 tenement building. Super-stylish rooms blend a minimalist aesthetic with natural woods, plus views from floor-to-ceiling windows.

🛈 145 🚇 A, C, E, to Canal St. 🅿️ All major cards

■ Gansevoort Meatpacking NYC
$$$$$
18 NINTH AVE. (BETWEEN LITTLE WEST 12TH AND 13TH STREETS)
TEL 212/206-6700
gansevoorthotelgroup.com
This 187-room hotel in the Meatpacking District offers spectacular views of the city and the Hudson River from its room balconies and 45-foot (13.7 m) heated rooftop pool. Guests can be pampered at the huge spa, sip cocktails in the Gansevoort Rooftop, savor Japanese cuisine in the Saishin by Kissaki, and spin around the city on the hotel's complimentary bicycles.

🛈 187 🚇 A, C, E, L to 14th St. 🅿️ All major cards

■ Roxy Hotel
$$$$$
2 SIXTH AVENUE
TEL 212/519-6600
roxyhotelnyc.com
With a grand atrium inspired by European cathedrals and mid-20th-century public buildings, the Roxy features a private screening room

that makes it a favorite of celebrities. The rooms combine modernist design with wood paneling. Be sure to have a drink or two in the bar to maximize your celebrity-spotting chances.

🛈 203 🚇 6 to Astor Pl. 🅿️ All major cards

■ Hotel Hugo
$$$
525 GREENWICH STREET
TEL 855-516-9183
hotelhugony.com
Steps away from Washington Square Park, this renovated, century-old hotel has art-deco-inspired rooms, an excellent restaurant, and a lobby bar where guests can take tea or try cocktails while making use of the Wi-Fi access.

🛈 22 🚇 C & E to Spring St.. 🍴 🅿️ All major cards

■ Washington Square Hotel
$$
103 WAVERLY PLACE (AT MACDOUGAL STREET)
TEL 212/777-9515 OR 800/222-0418
washingtonsquarehotel.com
Steps away from Washington Square Park, this renovated, century-old hotel has art deco-inspired rooms, an excellent restaurant, and a lobby bar where guests can take tea or try cocktails while making use of the Wi-Fi access.

🛈 180 🚇 A, B, C, D, E, F to W. 4th St 🍴 🅿️ All major cards

■ Chelsea Inn Hotel
$
46 WEST 17TH STREET

TEL 212/645-8989
chelseainn.com
A good budget option a short walk from Greenwich village, its compact rooms with exposed brick walls have simple yet modern décor. Some bathrooms are shared.
🛈 34 🅿 F to 14th St. 💳 AE, MC, V

MIDTOWN SOUTH

■ Refinery Hotel
$$$$$
63 WEST 38TH STREET
TEL 646/664-0310
refineryhotelnewyork.com
Refinement is a watchword at this smart contemporary hotel with yesteryear-inspired accents. Its Parker & Quinn restaurant and fashionable rooftop bar are popular Midtown refuges.
🛈 197 🅿 Times Square/42nd St. 💳 All major cards

■ Arlo Midtown
$$$-$$$$$
351 WEST 38TH STREET
TEL 212/343-7000
arlohotels.com
Elegant modernist-inspired interiors and plenty of luxe comforts offer a sublime refuge from the frenetic city. A gourmet Italian-American restaurant, café, plus rooftop garden-bar round out this appealing option.
🛈 489 🅿 A, C, E to 42nd St./Port Authority Terminal 🍴 💳 All major cards

■ The Standard, High Line
$$$$
848 WASHINGTON STREET
(AT 13TH STREET)
TEL 212/645-4646
standardhotels.com/high-line
It's all about the views at this André Balazs hotel, which straddles the High Line in the hip Meatpacking District, just one block from the Hudson River. The building's exterior is reminiscent of international-style landmarks like the UN building, while its streamlined rooms are 21st-century modern. All are angled to maximize the views.
🛈 337 🅿 A, C, E to 14th St. 💳 All major cards

■ Mondrian Park Avenue
$$$-$$$$
444 PARK AVENUE SOUTH
TEL 212/804-8880
sbe.com/hotels/mondrian/park-avenue
Light and airy guest rooms combine luxurious furnishing with whimsical décor and curated art in this très chic hotel from Philippe Starck. Sophisticates also get to enjoy The Vasper gourmet brasserie and rooftop lounge terrace.
🛈 189 🅿 6 to 33rd St. 🍴 💳 All major cards

■ The Evelyn
$$$-$$$$
7 EAST 27TH STREET (BETWEEN FIFTH AND MADISON AVENUES)
TEL 212/453-4040
theevelyn.com
This 100-year-old spot in the city's old "Tin Pan Alley" area (home to hit 1930s and '40s songwriters) caters to creative global travelers. Rooms range from shared-bathroom dorms to private rooms and suites. Updated and upgraded in 2018,
it fuses original Beaux Arts elements into a fresh avant-garde styling.
🛈 140 🅿 6, N, R to 28th St. 💳 AE, MC, V

■ Hotel Chelsea
$$$$
222 WEST 23RD STREET (BETWEEN SEVENTH AND EIGHTH AVENUES)
TEL 212/483-1010
hotelchelsea.com
The historic home of artists and writers has a cozy lobby filled with art. Recently refurbished, it exudes yesteryear luxe, including a surfeit of marble and velvet. It's definitely worth a look even if no rooms are available.
🛈 400 🅿 1 to 23rd St.; C, E to 23rd St. 🚇 Nearby 💳 All major cards

■ Kixby
$$$$
45 WEST 35TH STREET (BETWEEN FIFTH AND SIXTH AVENUES)
TEL 212/947-2500
kixby.com
Infused with centenary sophistication, this Midtown hotel is a thoroughly modern eye-pleaser. Deluxe guest rooms join forces with a roof terrace that has views of the nearby Empire State Building. Also available are a fitness center and restaurant. The main Midtown sights are just minutes away.
🛈 195 🅿 1, 2, 3 to 34th St. 🍴 💳 All major cards

MIDTOWN NORTH

■ The Algonquin
$$$$$
59 WEST 44TH STREET (BETWEEN

FIFTH AND SIXTH AVENUES)
TEL 212/840-6800
algonquinhotel.com
This official literary landmark
has been entertaining writers
since the 1920s. Enjoy the
glamour of the Round Table
restaurant and cocktails in the
Lobby Lounge The rooms are
charming, the locale is ideal,
and all guests' needs are noted
for the next visit.
🛈 175 🚇 B, D, F to 42nd St.
💳 All major cards

■ **Four Seasons**
$$$$$
57 EAST 57TH STREET (BETWEEN
PARK AND MADISON AVENUES)
TEL 212/758-5700
fourseasons.com/newyork
This 52-story, art deco–style
monument designed by I. M.
Pei and completed in 1993 has
received top ratings and boasts
the largest rooms in the city,
with accompanying big views.
Expect modernistic furniture,
giant Florentine marble
bathrooms, and elaborate
bedside push-button systems.
🛈 370 🚇 4, 5, 6, N, R to 59th St.
🍴 💳 All major cards

■ **JW Marriott Essex
House**
$$$$$
160 CENTRAL PARK SOUTH
(BETWEEN SIXTH AND SEVENTH
AVENUES)
TEL 212/247-0300 OR
800-228-9290
marriott.com
Essex House completed a
$90-million refurbishment
in late 2017 that conserved
its dramatic art deco setting
and added high-tech,
environmentally friendly

features. The hotel has stunning
views of Central Park.
🛈 426 rooms + 101 suites 🚇 1, A,
C, B, D to Columbus Circle–59th St.;
N, R, Q to 57th St. 🍴
💳 All major cards

■ **The Knickerbocker**
$$$$$
6 TIMES SQUARE
TEL 212/204-4980
theknickerbocker.com
Once home to the Rockefellers,
and host to many an actress,
tycoon, and political bigwig, this
once stately historic hotel in the
heart of Times Square has been
rehabbed with a super chic
modern vogue. Master Chef
Charlie Palmer oversees The
Knick restaurant.
🛈 330 🚇 Times Square 🍴
🚌 💳 All major cards

■ **The Peninsula**
$$$$$
700 FIFTH AVENUE
(AT 55TH STREET)
TEL 212/956-2888
peninsula.com
A turn-of-the-20th-century
beaux arts landmark offers
views down Fifth Avenue,
art nouveau furnishings, and
oversized beds and bathrooms.
More luxury awaits at the
rooftop spa and outdoor
rooftop Salon de Ning,
excellent for summer-time
cocktails and city views.
🛈 250 🚇 E, V to 5th Ave./53rd
St.; F to 57th St. 🍴 🚌 💳 All
major cards

■ **The Plaza**
$$$$$
CENTRAL PARK SOUTH
768 FIFTH AVENUE
(AT 59TH STREET)

TEL 212/759-3000
theplazany.com
The iconic luxury hotel's 282
suites and rooms include
the suite where the beloved
children's book character Eloise
has "lived" since 1955. The
Grand Ballroom, Palm Court
(with Tiffany ceiling), Oak
Room, and Oak Bar are among
its historic features, and guests
should make a point of strolling
the exterior grounds at the
corner of Central Park.
🛈 282 🚇 N, R to 5th Ave./
59th St. 🍴 💳 All major cards

■ **The Ritz-Carlton**
$$$$$
50 CENTRAL PARK SOUTH
(AT SIXTH AVENUE)
TEL 212/308-9100 OR
800/241-3333
marriott.com
Recently redesigned
in townhouse-inspired
contemporary styling, this
33-story luxury hotel offers
glamour, a great location,
butlers, and fabulous lounges.
The Contour restaurant serves
innovative American cuisine.
🛈 261 🚇 F to 57th St. 🍴
💳 All major cards

■ **St. Regis**
$$$$$
2 EAST 55TH STREET (BETWEEN
FIFTH AND MADISON AVENUES)
TEL 212/753-4500
marriott.com
This restored 1904 beaux
arts gem has regal guest
rooms, several elegant yet
accessible public rooms, and
the finest service and amenities
throughout. Don't miss the
great King Cole Bar, dominated

by the engaging Maxfield
Parrish mural of the monarch
himself.

ⓘ *322* E, V, to 5th Ave./53rd
St.; N, R to 5th Ave./59th St.
All major cards

■ The Shoreham
$$$$$
33 WEST 55TH STREET (BETWEEN
FIFTH AND SIXTH AVENUES)
TEL 212/632-9070
shorehamhotel.com
A lavish refurbishment of
this pet-friendly boutique hotel
has created individually styled
rooms with slate and marble
bathrooms and fitness center.
ⓘ *47 + 37 suites* E, V to 5th
Ave./53rd St.; N, Q, R to 57th
St./7th Ave. Nearby
All major cards

■ The Waldorf-Astoria & Waldorf Towers
$$$$$
301 PARK AVENUE
(AT 50TH STREET)
TEL 212/355-3000
waldorftowers.nyc
The great Waldorf-Astoria
is one of the quintessential
New York hotels. The art
deco lobby is magnificent,
and the elaborately appointed
Waldorf Towers (floors 28–42)
provide quarters for every
visiting president from Herbert
Hoover to Barack Obama. A
$1 billion conversion launched
in 2021 to reimagine the hotel
and convert the Towers into
deluxe condominiums and is
expected to be completed
by 2024.
ⓘ *375* 6 to 51st St. or E, V to
Lexington Ave./53rd St.
All major cards

■ Casablanca Hotel
$$$$-$$$$$
147 WEST 43RD STREET
(BETWEEN SIXTH AVENUE AND
BROADWAY)
TEL 212/869-1212
casablancahotel.com
They're serious about the
name, with Moroccan touches
mixing with modern, a lounge
called Rick's Café, and a
vaguely North African outdoor
courtyard. This hotel is great
for theatergoers.
ⓘ *40 + 8 suites* 1, 2, 3, 7 to
Times Sq.–42nd St. All
major cards

■ W New York
$$$$
1567 BROADWAY
TEL 212/930-7400
wnewyorktimessquare.com
A massive Pop Art–style mural
plus a dance and live-music
area set the tone for this
hip, party-hearty hotel with
ultra-chic décor, seafood and
Mexican restaurants, plus and
a sensational bar.
ⓘ *509* 49nd St All
major cards

■ Millennium Hilton New York One UN Hotel
$$$-$$$$
1 UNITED NATIONS PLAZA 44TH
STREET (BETWEEN FIRST AND
SECOND AVENUES)
TEL 212/758-1234
hilton.com
The twin-towered modern
building rises high above the
East Side. Staying here puts you
in the midst of global drama,
as diplomats and staff rush to
meetings or to their offices on
the first 27 floors of the UN
Plaza. Hotel rooms—all with
stunning views—start on the
28th floor. Artworks from New
York City and various nations are
found throughout the hotel. The
excellent sports facilities include
a fitness center. A shuttle services
major city sites and the airports.
ⓘ *439* G4, 5, 6, 7 to 42nd St.
All major cards

■ Lotte New York Palace
$$$$$
455 MADISON AVENUE
(AT 50TH STREET)
TEL 212/888-7000 OR
800/804-7035
lottenypalace.com
Located in what was originally
the 1882 Stanford White–
designed Villard Houses, this
landmark site has retained
its opulence through various
incarnations. Its elegantly
furnished 55-story tower
overlooks St. Patrick's Cathedral.
Fine places for food and drink
on-site include the lavish,
medieval-style Gold Room.
ⓘ *600* E, F to 5th Ave.;
B, D, F to Rockefeller Center
All major cards

■ The Paramount
$$$$
235 WEST 46TH STREET
(BETWEEN BROADWAY
AND EIGTH AVENUE)
TEL 212/764-5500 OR
877-692-0803
nycparamount.com
A Philippe Starck–designed
lobby, playful, minimalist decor,
and location in the heart of
the theater district are among
this hotel's pluses. Try for one of
the recently renovated rooms.
ⓘ *601 + 12 suites* 1, 2, 3, 7
to 42nd St.–Times Sq. All
major cards

TRAVEL ESSENTIALS

Hotel Elysée

$$$$$

60 EAST 54TH STREET
(BETWEEN MADISON
AND PARK AVENUES)
TEL 212/753-1066
elyseehotel.com

Thirties' decor, charming
rooms, a small roof terrace,
and evening wine and cheese
in a sumptuous lounge make
this boutique hotel both
luxurious and personal.

📋 88 + 11 suites 🚇 E to Lexington
Ave.; 6 to 51st St. 📺 💳 All major
cards

UPPER EAST SIDE

The Carlyle

$$$$$

35 EAST 76TH STREET
TEL 212/744-1600
rosewoodhotels.com

Since 1931, this gemlike hotel
has welcomed the world's
elite in a grand European
style. Rooms have antiques,
marble bathrooms with
whirlpools, and state-of-the-
art electronics. Nancy Reagan
and the late President John F.
Kennedy were regular guests.
Those who do not check in
may still partake of romantic
dining in the Dowlings at The
Carlyle, bistro entertainment
in the Café Carlyle, cocktails
in Bemelmans Bar, or tea in
the Gallery, modeled after
Istanbul's Topkapi Palace, in
Turkey.

📋 190 + 65 residential apartments
🚇 6 to 77th St 💳 All major cards

The Lowell

$$$$$

28 EAST 63RD STREET (BETWEEN
PARK AND MADISON AVENUE)
TEL 212/838-1400
lowellhotel.com

This 1920s historic landmark
on a quiet street provides
tasteful, Old World charm
in an intimate setting. Many
rooms have working fireplaces,
kitchens, and libraries.

📋 74 🚇 4, 5, 6 to 59th St. 📺
💳 All major cards

The Mark

$$$$$

25 EAST 77TH STREET (BETWEEN
FIFTH AND MADISON AVENUES)
TEL 212/744-4300 OR
866/744-4300
themarkhotel.com

In an elegant location , this
hotel features formal decor,
large rooms with marble or
ceramic baths, high-quality
artwork, and luxurious
amenities. The wood-paneled
The Mark Restaurant by
Jean-Georges is perfect for
indulgent afternoon teas.

📋 180 🚇 6 to 77th St. 📺
💳 All major cards

The Pierre

$$$$$

2 EAST 61ST STREET
(AT FIFTH AVENUE)
TEL 212/838-8000
thepierreny.com

Elegance, antiques, and
opulent decor characterize this
hotel overlooking Central Park
that dates from the 1930s.
Rooms are high-ceilinged
and decorated in cool, restful
colors, with furnishings in rich
silks and brocades.

📋 186 🚇 N, R to 5th Ave. 📺
💳 All major cards

Loews Regency New York

$$$$$

540 PARK AVENUE
(AT 61ST STREET)
TEL 212/759-4100 OR
877-878-6204
loewshotels.com

Named for its original Regency
decor, this hotel has been
recently updated with a suave,
contemporary vibe and boasts
both understated elegance and
every amenity, including TVs
and phones beside the marble
bathtubs.

📋 288 + 74 suites 🚇 4, 5, 6 to
59th St. 📺 💳 All major cards

The Sherry-Netherland

$$$$$

781 FIFTH AVENUE (AT 59TH
STREET)
TEL 212/355-2800 OR
877/743-7710
sherrynetherland.com

This exclusive 1927 apartment
hotel at the edge of Central
Park numbers among its many
attractions a lobby modeled
on the Vatican library and
guest elevators that once
graced the Vanderbilt Mansion.
Suites include separate living
and dining areas. The fitness
center is state-of-the-art, and
a recent renovation injected
the legendary restaurant, Harry
Cipriani, with a new look.

📋 53 🚇 N, R to 5th Ave./
59th St. 💳 All major cards

The Franklin Hotel

$$$-$$$$

164 EAST 87TH STREET (BETWEEN
LEXINGTON AND THIRD
AVENUES)
TEL 212/369-1000
franklinhotel.com

Pet friendly and romantic,

this understated hotel in a handsome brownstone offers nicely decorated rooms with custom contemporary furniture. There are complimentary wine-and-cheese receptions nightly.

ⓘ 53 🚇 4, 5, 6 to 86th St. 💳 AE, MC, V

■ Fitzpatrick Manhattan
$$$
687 LEXINGTON AVE., BTWN 56TH & 57TH STS.
TEL 212/355-0100
fitzpatrickhotels.com
This Irish-themed hotel boutique brings a subtle and modern Irish country house touch to Manhattan, with comfy and charming rooms and 24-hour room service. Tuck into Irish fare in the ground floor Fitz Restaurant. Guests get access to a fitness center.

ⓘ 91 🚇 Lexington Ave. and 62rd 💳 All major cards

■ Bentley Hotel
$$-$$$$
500 E. 52ND STREET
TEL 212/644-6000
bentleyhotelnyc.com
This chic boutique hideaway radiates New York City style while offering sprawling views of the Queensboro Bridge and New York skyline from elegant contemporary guestrooms. Nearby First Avenue offers good dining options.

ⓘ 197 🚇 E to Lexington Ave./53rd St. 🍽 💳 All major cards

UPPER WEST SIDE

■ Mandarin Oriental
$$$$$
80 COLUMBUS CIRCLE
TEL 212/805-8800

mandarinoriental.com
A statement to good taste, this luxury hotel atop Deutsche Bank Center offers spectacular views through floor-to-ceiling windows in regally appointed guestrooms with oriental flair. Indulge in the spa and lap pool, and dine in its MO Lounge.

ⓘ 244 🚇 66th St./Lincoln Center 🍽 💳 All major cards

■ Arthouse Hotel
$$$
2178 BROADWAY AT WEST 57TH S
arthousehotelnyc.com
Steps from the American Museum of Natural History, the hotel offers loft-style rooms with floor-to-ceiling windows and eye-pleasing minimalist furnishings. Rotating art exhibitions and live music in the wine bar are additional draws.

ⓘ 291 🚇 79th St. 💳 All major cards

■ Hotel Beacon NYC
$$$
2130 BROADWAY (AT 75TH STREET)
TEL 212/787-1100 OR 800/572-4969
beaconhotel.com
Generously sized rooms, a great central location, and a family-friendly ethos characterize this hotel. All rooms and suites have marble bathrooms and fully equipped kitchenettes.

ⓘ 248 suites 🚇 1, 2, 3 to 72nd St. 🍽 Nearby 💳 All major cards

■ The Lucerne
$$$
201 WEST 79TH STREET (AT AMSTERDAM AVENUE)
TEL 212/875-1000 OR 800/492-8122
thelucernehotel.com

Classic rooms in a gorgeously renovated 1904 landmark building combine with a location close to Central Park and a popular restaurant and sidewalk café frequented by locals. Guests can enjoy the complimentary wine hour on Thursday evenings.

ⓘ 184 🚇 1 to 79th St. 💳 AE, MC, V

■ The Hotel Newton
$-$$
2528 BROADWAY
TEL 212/678-6500
thehotelnewton.com
Comfortable guest rooms include deluxe suites with kitchenettes. The location of the hotel is excellent for prime sightseeing and strolls to Riverside and Central Parks. Friendly staff will help with queries and bookings. Dining options abound, the nearest being the Manhattan Diner next door.

ⓘ 117 🚇 1,2,3 to 96th St.

HARLEM

■ Aloft Harlem
$$-$$$$
2296 FREDERICK DOUGLASS BLVD
TEL 212/749-4000
aloft-hotels.marriott.com
This colorful, hip, uber-contemporary design-led hotel is environmentally friendly and features oversize artwork in guest rooms. In the heart of Harlem, it's mere steps from six subway lines and such iconic restaurants as Sylvia's and Red Rooster.

ⓘ 122 🚇 125th St. 💳 All major cards

TRAVEL ESSENTIALS

■ Northern Lights Mansion

$$-$$$$

210 WEST 122ND STREET
TEL 212/866-4411
northernlightsmansion.com

A quintessential bed-and-breakfast in a beautifully restored 1880 brownstone manse, this luxury option feels like a true home-from-home. A short walk from the Apollo Theatre and major subways.

3 rooms + 3 suites *125th St. at Malcolm X Blvd.* *MC, V*

■ Central Park North

$$

137 WEST 111TH ST.
TEL 212/662-2300
central-park-north.com

Inside a newly renovated 19th-century brownstone just steps from Central Park, this cozy bargain-priced inn has soothing contemporary décor, although guests must share bathrooms.

12 *Central Park North and 110th St.*
MC, V

BROOKLYN

■ Wythe Hotel

$$$$$

80 Wythe Ave.
TEL 718/460-8000
wythehotel.com

The ultimate hipster experience is guaranteed at this industrial-chic waterfront hotel (think custom-made furniture, exposed brick walls, and killer Manhattan views). Fabulous meals and beautiful people await at Le Crocodile, the restaurant that is housed in the hotel's street level.

70 *L to Bedford Ave., G to Nassau Ave.* *All major cards*

■ New York Marriott at the Brooklyn Bridge

$$$$$

333 ADAMS STREET
TEL 718/246-7000
marriott.com

A luxury hotel just across the river from Lower Manhattan. Situated close to the Brooklyn Bridge near the historic Brooklyn Heights neighborhood.

638 + 28 suites *A, C, F to Jay St.* *All major cards*

■ 1 Hotel Brooklyn Bridge

$$$

60 FURMAN STREET
TEL 347/696 2500
1hotels.com/brooklyn-bridge

A prime location at Pier 1 just south of the iconic bridge, elegant contemporary furnishings, plus a wellness spa and signature restaurant make a winning combo.

194 *High St./Brooklyn Bridge* *All major cards*

AIRPORT HOTELS

■ City View Inn

$$$

3317 GREENPOINT AVENUE, LONG ISLAND CITY
TEL 718/392-8400
cityviewinn.net

This converted 19th-century public school is near the New York Mets' Citi Field stadium and U.S Open Tennis Center. Free shuttle to and from LaGuardia.

72 *7 to 40th Street*

Nearby *All major cards*

■ Sheraton LaGuardia East Hotel

$$$

135-20 39TH AVENUE
TEL 718/460-6666 OR 800/325-3535
marriott.com

Modern airport hotel near the U.S. Open Tennis Center and the Mets' Citi Field.

173 suites *7 to Main St. Flushing* *All major cards*

INDEX

INDEX

Authors

Katherine Cancila

Additional text by Lisa Armstrong, Eleanor Berman, Christina Cush, Margie Goldsmith, Diana Greenwald, Randy Hecht, Rob Kimmel, Judy Kirkwood, Marni Kleinfield-Hayes, Chris Michel, Linda Tagliaferro, Sarah Wolf, Joe Yogerst, Cristi Young

Picture Credits

t = top; b = bottom, l = left; r = right, m = middle

2-3 Alex Segre/Alamy. 4 Amanda Hall/Robert Harding Travel/photolibrary.com. 5tr Michelle Bennett/Lonely Planet Images. 5bl Courtesy of Jeanne M.Beaumon/Museum of the City of New York/MCNY02/The Art Archive. 5mr Alan Gallery/Alamy. 6 Jean-Pierre Lescourret/Imagebroker.net/photolibrary. 9 Wayne Fodgen/Ticket/photolibrary.com. 12-13 Ilja Mašík/Shutterstock. 14l Ramin Talaie/Corbis. 14r Bildagenturm/Tips Italia/photolibrary.com. 15 Frances M.Roberts/Alamy. 16 Michael S.Yamashita/Corbis. 18r Radius Images/photolibrary.com. 18l Sam Chadwick/Shutterstock. 19l Songquan Deng/Dreamstime.com. 19r Cedric Weber/Shutterstock. 20 Richard Levine/Alamy. 21l Tony Savino/Corbis. 21r fotog/Tetra Images/photolibrary.com. 22 Bertrand Gardel/Hemis/photolibrary.com. 24l Natalija Sirokova/Shutterstock. 24r Stock Connection Blue/Alamy. 25tl Dimitrios Kambouris/ Getty Images. 25tr Supri Shuharjoto/Shutterstock. 25b Andria Patino/Age fotostock/photolibrary.com. 26 Len Holsborg/Alamy. 28tl Scholastic. 28tr Ramin Talaie/Corbis. 28l New York City Fire Museum. 29l lazyllama/Shutterstock. 29r Sepavo/Dreamstime.com. 31 Children's Museum of the Arts. 32l Copyright of johnabbottphoto.com. 32r Mark & Audrey Gibson/photolibrary. 33 Shutterstock customers love this asset!/Shutterstock. 34 Leonard Zhukovsky / Shutterstock. 36-37 Giuseppe Masci/Tips Italia/photolibrary.com. 40 Cameron Davidson/Corbis. 42m The National Museum of the American Indian. 42b Caitlin Mirra/Shutterstock. 43 dbimages/Alamy. 45 Photo Equipe 153/Cuboimages/photolibrary.com. 47 Ben Pipe/Ticket/photolibrary.com. 49 sevapo/Shutterstock. 50 Library of Congress. 52 Keiko Niwa, courtesy Lower East Side Tenement Museum. 53 Michael S.Yamashita/Corbis. 55 Dan Herrick/Lonely Planet Images. 56 Walter Weissman/Corbis. 58tl Peter Bennett/Ambient Images/photolibrary.com. 58bl James Leynse/Corbis. 59t AA World Travel Library/Alamy. 59mr Merchant's House Museum. 60 Dan Herrick/Lonely Planet Images. 63 Justin Lane/epa/Corbis. 64 Eye Ubiquitous/photolibrary.com.66 Allen Ginsberg/Corbis. 67 Neville Elder/Corbis. 69 Larry Busacca/Getty Images. 70 Hermann Dobler/Imagebroker.net/photolibrary.com. 72tl Rubin Museum of Art, C2006.41.1 (HAR 65692. 72bl Songquan Deng/Shutterstock. 73tr Rafael Macia/Ticket/photolibrary.com. 73br Jim Zuckerman/Flirt Collection/photolibrary.com. 75 Barry Winiker/Ticket/photolibrary.com. 76 Richard Cummins/Robert Harding Travel/photolibrary.com. 79 Vittorio Sciosia/Cuboimages/photolibrary.com. 80 RosalreneBetancourt9/Alamy. 82 Jutta Klee/FStop/photolibrary.com. 83 Ludovic Maisant/Hemis/photolibrary.com. 85 Jin Lee/Bloomberg/Getty Images. 86 Andrew F.Kazmierski/Shutterstock. 88t Jorg Hackemann/Shutterstock. 88b Timothy A Clary/AFP/Getty Images. 89 Marcin Wasilewski/Shutterstock. 91 Andrey Bayda/Shutterstock. 92 Songquan Deng/Shutterstock. 95 Tetra Images/photolibrary.com. 96 Kordcom/Age fotostock/photolibrary.com. 98 Ambient Images Inc./Superstock. 99 Mishella/Shutterstock. 101 Richard Green/Alamy 102 Michelle Bennett/Lonely Planet Images. 104tr Courtesy of Jeanne M.Beaumon/Museum of the City of New York/MCNY02/The Art Archive. 104bl Christian Kober/Robert Harding Travel/photolibrary.com. 104tl Jeff Greenherg/photolibrary.com. 105r Rudi Von Briel/photolibrary.com. 105l Tom Pepeira/Iconotec/photolibrary .com. 106 Bryan Bedder/Getty Images. 108 Christian Kober/Robert Harding Travel/photolibrary.com. 111 Peter Bennett/Ambient Images/photolibrary.com. 112 Herman Dobler/Imagebroker.net/photolibrary.com. 114 Barry Winiker/Ticket/photolibrary.com. 116 Mama Bear by Tom Otterness, On view at Marlborough Gallery, booth 402, Pier 92/Image credit: David Willems, Courtesy of The Armory Show. 117 Pieter Schoolwerth, *Your Vacuum Blows,* *which Sucks,* Miguel Abreu Gallery, New York, 2015; Installation view; Courtesy the artist and Miguel Abreu Gallery. 119 Ingolf Pompe/LOOK-foto/photolibrary.com. 120 Jean-Pierre Lescourret/Superstock/photolibrary.com. 122m John A.Anderson/Shutterstock. 122b Richard A.McGuirk/Shutterstock. 123mr redswept/Shutterstock. 123bm Gail Mooney/Corbis. 125 eddie-hernandez.com/Shutterstock. 127 Sandra Baker/Alamy. 128 Spencer Grant/Alamy. 129 Paramount/The Kobal Collection. 131 Demetrio Carrasco/JAI/Corbis. 132 Frances Roberts/Alamy.134r Francesco Tomasinelli/Tips Italia/photolibrary.com. 134l Jeff Greenberg/Age fotostock/photolibrary.com. 135tl © Collection of the New-York Historical Society, USA/The Bridgeman Art Library. 135br Mike Liu/Shutterstock. 135bl Barry Winiker/Ticket/photolibrary.com. 136 © Collection of the New-York Historical Society, USA/The Bridgeman Art Library. 138 sepavo/Shutterstock.com. 140 Renaud Visage/Age fotostock/photolibrary.com. 142 Gregory James Van Raalte/Shutterstock. 143 Colin D.Young/Shutterstock. 145 Andrew Pini/Fresh Food Images/photolibrary .com. 146 Barry Winiker/photolibrary .com. 148 Morris-Jumel Mansion. 149tl Thos Robinson/Getty Images. 149bl Dave Bowman/Alamy. 149br P.Deliss/Godong/Corbis. 150 La Cama (The Bed), 1987 by Pepón Osorio, Mixed Media Installation, Collection El Museo del Barrio, New York. 152 Peter Bennett/Ambient Images/photolibrary .com. 154 William Manning/Alamy. 156 Courtesy, The Lilly Library, Indiana University, Bloomington, Indiana. 157 Frank Driggs Collection/Getty Images. 158 Bill Wassman/Lonely Planet Images. 160t SVLuma/Shutterstock. 160b Alan Gallery/Alamy. 161t Brooklyn Museum. 161br Rick Shupper/Ambient Images/photolibrary.com. 163 Mark Peterson/Corbis. 164 Jackie Weisberg/Ambient Images/photolibrary. 167 Thistle Hill Tavern. 168 Brooklyn Museum. 170 Tobbe/Corbis. 171 Ron Chapple Stock/photolibrary.com. 173 Vladimir Korostyshevskiy/Shutterstock. 174-175 Allan Baxter/Photodisc/Getty Images.

Walking New York
Katherine Cancila

Since 1888, the National Geographic Society has funded more than 14,000 research, conservation, education, and storytelling projects around the world. National Geographic Partners distributes a portion of the funds it receives from your purchase to National Geographic Society to support programs including the conservation of animals and their habitats.

National Geographic Partners, LLC
1145 17th Street NW
Washington, DC 20036-4688 USA

Get closer to National Geographic explorers and photographers, and connect with our global community. Join us today at nationalgeographic.org/joinus

For rights or permissions inquiries, please contact National Geographic Books Subsidiary Rights: bookrights@natgeo.com

Edition edited by White Star s.r.l.
Licensee of National Geographic Partners, LLC.
Update by Christopher P. Baker

The information in this book has been carefully checked and to the best of our knowledge is accurate. However, details are subject to change, and the publisher cannot be responsible for such changes, or for errors or omissions. Assessments of sites, hotels, and restaurants are based on the author's subjective opinions, which do not necessarily reflect the publisher's opinion.

ISBN: 978-8-8544-1968-1

Printed In China

23/TL/1

MIX
Paper from
responsible sources
FSC® C178000